SCOTS
in the
AMERICAN WEST
1783–1883

by
David Dobson

CLEARFIELD

Printed for
Clearfield Company, Inc. by
Genealogical Publishing Co., Inc.
Baltimore, Maryland
2003

International Standard Book Number: 0-8063-5198-5

Made in the United States of America

INTRODUCTION

The American West was an ever-changing concept. At the close of the American Revolution in 1783, the West lay beyond the Wabash and the Mississippi Rivers. It was largely an area claimed by Spain but partly territory claimed by both Great Britain and the United States. The catchment area of this book lies west of a line from Detroit to New Orleans, roughly following the Wabash, Ohio, and Mississippi Rivers, to the Pacific Ocean. The Louisiana Purchase of 1803 vastly extended the area of American jurisdiction, as did the Annexation of Texas in 1845 followed by the War Against Mexico 1846-1848. In less than a century the size of the United States had more than trebled in land area.

Scots, specifically trappers, traders and soldiers could be found in the Ohio Valley before 1783, but they were few in number. However, the opening up of the West necessitated large scale migration and settlement both from the eastern states and from Europe. Newspapers in Europe were used to promote emigration to the American West as the following extract from the Glasgow Herald, #4066, dated 17 January 1842 attests.

"Emigration to Texas, North America.

A vessel with emigrants is intended to sail from the Clyde for Texas in the course of the next month. Persons availing themselves of this opportunity will receive grants of land on very advantageous terms.
The salubrious climate of Texas with the rich productiveness and soil clear and unencomered by forests present unusual advantages to the settler, above all to small farmers and to the rural population of Scotland of industrious habits and limited capital who might in that country place themselves at once in comfort and independence.
The grants of land being to a limited extent, early applicants will have a preference.

Texas opens up a new and promising market for shippers of goods.

Macgoun and Paterson, 41 Virginia Street, Glasgow.
14 January 1842"

Economic opportunities in the American West attracted substantial capital investment by Scottish companies in a range of industries, including mining, sheep and cattle ranching, railways, land, and timber, which in turn led to Scottish settlement in the West. In 1825 the British Government repealed the laws restricting the emigration of skilled industrial workers, which enabled Scots tradesmen emigrate to America freely. These men, however, mostly settled in the growing industrial towns of the east and the mid-west of the United States. Those who headed west beyond the Mississippi were mainly farmers attracted by the availability of land. The other major factors influencing the decision to settle in the West were religion and the discovery of gold in California. While the majority of emigrants from Scotland landed in Atlantic ports, some voyaged to New Orleans and then up the Mississippi to St. Louis, and a few sailed directly for San Francisco, before commencing their overland journeys. By the end of our period Scots could be found in every western state and territory.

This compilation identifies a number of these Scottish pioneers and is overwhelmingly based on primary source material located in Scotland, especially from contemporary newspapers but also from archival sources.

David Dobson
St Andrews, Scotland, 2002.

REFERENCES

ANY=Bio. Register of St Andrew's Society of New York
AO   =Annandale Observer, series
AOSC   =Annals of the Original Secession Church,
            D. Scott,   [Edinburgh, 1886]
AJ   =Aberdeen Journal, series
BL   =British Library, London
CM   = Caledonian Mercury, series
DA   =Dundee Advertiser, series
DGC   =Dumfries & Galloway Courier, series
DGH   =Dumfries & Galloway Herald, series
DJ   =Dunfermline Journal, series
DRTL   =Daughters of the Republic of Texas Library
EA   =Edinburgh Advertiser, series
EC   =Edinburgh Courant, series
EFR   =East Fife Record, series
ENES   =Emigration from North East Scotland,
            M. Harper,[Aberdeen, 1988]
EC   = Edinburgh Courant, series
EEC   =Edinburgh Evening Courant, series
EUL   =Edinburgh University Library
F   =Fasti Ecclesiae Scoticanae, [Edinburgh 1915]
FCP   =Families of California Pioneers
FFP   =Fife Free Press, series
FH   =Fife Herald, series
FJ   =Fife Journal, series
FPF   =Four Perthshire Families, [Edinburgh 1887]
GA   =Glasgow Archives
GaGaz   =Georgia Gazette, series
GM   =Gentleman's Magazine, series
GRH   =General Register House, Edinburgh
IGS   =Iowa Genealogical Society
LGS   =Louisiana Genealogical Society
MCA   =Marischal College, Aberdeen
NAS   =National Archives of Scotland, Edinburgh
NRH   =New Register House, Edinburgh
IC   =Inverness Courier, series
IGS   = Iowa Genealogical Society
OCGS   = Orange County Genealogical Society
PJ   =People's Journal, series
PR   =Pittenweem Register, series
RGG   =Roll of Graduates of the University of Glasgow,
            1727-1897, W.I.Addison, [Glasgow, 1898]
S   =Scotsman [6.7.2001]
SAUL   =St Andrews University Library
SFL   =San Francisco Ship Passenger Lists
SG   =Scottish Guardian, series
SHR   =Scottish Historical Review, series

SM	=Scots Magazine, series
TSHA	=Texas State Historical Association
UGL	=University of Glasgow Library
UPC	= Annals of the United Presbyterian Church, [Edinburgh, 1873]
USNA	=United States National Archives
W	=Witness, series
WSP	=Washington State Pioneers
1812	=British Aliens in USA, 1812. [Baltimore, 1979]

Abbreviations

Cnf	=	confirmation of testament
G/s	=	gravestone inscription
Inv	=	inventory
OPR	=	Old Parish Register
PCC	=	Prerogative Court of Canterbury

SCOTS IN THE AMERICAN WEST, 1783-1883

ABERDEIN, JAMES, born in 1807, from Dundee, died in Jefferson
County, Indiana, in 1881. [S#11,784]

ADAM, JAMES, from Glasgow, in Illinois before 1833.
[NAS.SH.28.2.1833]

ADAM, KENNETH, son of John Adam late of the Prince of Wales
Tavern, Glasgow, died in New Orleans in August 1831.
[GkAd#3818]

ADAM, ROBERT, from Glasgow, died in Randolph County,
Illinois, before 1853. [NAS.SH.28.2.1853]

AFFLECK, THOMAS, born in Dumfries on 13 July 1812, son of
Thomas Affleck and his wife Mary Hannay, educated at
Edinburgh University, arrived in USA 4 May 1832, married
Anna Dunbar Smith in Washington, Mississippi, 1842,
planter, nurseyman and writer, settled in Texas 1858, died 30
December 1868 in Glenbyther, Brenham, Texas.
[TSHA#14/0.547]

AINSLIE, JOHN, of Marpoffle, an advocate, died in Boonsville,
Missouri, on 13 June 1841. [EEC#20192]

AITCHISON, Waldie or Parkinson, Mrs **ELLIOT,** born 1819, from
Kelso and Galashiels, Roxburghshire, died in Centralia,
Illinois, on 15 July 1877. [S#10,621]

AITCHISON, Dr GEORGE, born 1810, eldest son of James
Aitchison, Oldcastles, Berwickshire, died in Reno, Nevada,
on 6 July 1882, cnf Edinburgh 1901.
[NAS.SC70.1.406/820][S#12,184]

AITCHISON, JOHN HOOD, Gardner, Illinois, married Jane
Gregson, daughter of Anthony Gregson, Essex, Kankakee,
there on 25 January 1872. [S#9202]

AITCHISON, ROBERT, born 1863, from Bridgend, Eyemouth,
Berwickshire, died in Janesville, Wisconsin, on 2 September
1882. [S#12,228]

AITKEN, ROBERT, eldest son of John Aitken, Fingland, Eskdalemuir, Dumfries-shire, died in Golden Prairie, USA, on 29 July 1872. [AO]

AITKIN, WILLIAM, born in 1814, a farmer from Friershaw, died on Dale Farm, Paullina, Iowa, 15 May 1891. [Lilliesleaf g/s, Roxburghshire]

ALEXANDER, ALEXANDER SEPTIMUS, late of 4 Bellevue Terrace, Kelvinside, Glasgow, now of Chicago, Illinois, married Mary Frances Hope, daughter of Joseph Hope, Cushathill, Ecclefechan, Dumfries-shire, in Edinburgh on 5 January 1887. [AO: 7.1.1887]

ALEXANDER, ANDREW SNODGRASS MUIR, in Chicago by 1889, nephew of George Lewis William Forbes a solicitor in Banff. [NAS.SH.5.2.1889]

ALEXANDER, DENHAM, eldest daughter of George Alexander, Woodstock, Upper Canada, died in Sacramento, California, on 17 June 1873. [S#9351]

ALEXANDER, ..., daughter of A. S. Alexander, was born in Fullersburg, Illinois, on 18 October 1887. [AO:4.11.1887]

ALEXANDER, DAVID GRAY, born in 1812, son of Robert Alexander, died in Virginia City, California, on 30 July 1862. [Ayton g/s, Berwickshire]

ALLAN, JAMES, born in 1849, son of Alexander Allan [1802-1869], died in Chicago on 27 November 1876. [Whithorn Old g/s]

ALLAN, JOHN, son of Robert Allan in Kirkintilloch, Dunbartonshire, settled in Richfield, Utah, before 1874. [NAS.SH.23.3.1878]

ALLAN, MAGGIE, eldest daughter of Peter Allan, from Bathgate, West Lothian, married Hilton Middleton in Lynville, Illinois, on 16 February 1875.[EC#28474]

ALLAN, WILLIAM, born 1839, a stonecutter from Crieff, Perthshire, died at the residence of his brother James Allan, Baxter, Gaspar County, Iowa, on 28 May 1879. [S#11,207]

ALLARDYCE, ROBERT ALEXANDER, in Amboy, Illinois, by 1890, son of Robert Allardyce a merchant in Calcutta who died 24 June 1869. [NAS.SH.4.10.1890]

ALLISON, JAMES, son of John Allan in Paisley, Renfrewshire, settled in Wisconsin before 1850. [NAS.SH.31.8.1852]

ALLISON, JAMES, an auctioneer from Dumfries, died in Texas on 2 August 1876. [AO]

ANCRUM, GEORGE, in Louisiana by 23 February 1764. [GaGaz#47]

ANDERSON, ALEXANDER, a mason in Will County, Illinois, died in February 1860. [NAS.SH.18.7.1877]

ANDERSON, ALEXANDER JOHNSTON, a stonecutter, late of New York, died in California on 30 December 1876. [S#10,458]

ANDERSON, ANDREW, born in 1841, son of Andrew Anderson, a painter in Aberdeen, died in Chicago on 17 August 1872. [AJ:11.9.1872]

ANDERSON, CURTIS HOME, born in 1852, son of Dr Anderson of Jedburgh, Roxburghshire, and of China, died in Las Vegas, New Mexico, in 1883. [EC#30995][S#12,647]

ANDERSON, DAVID WILSON, born in 1827, son of William Anderson [1792-1876], killed in a goldmine in California on 15 June 1867. [Mochrum g/s, Wigtownshire]

ANDERSON, EBENEZER, from Cupar, Fife, a farmer in Detroit, Michigan, cnf 1892 Edinburgh. [NAS.SC70.1.307]

ANDERSON, EDGAR, in Schuyler, Illinois, cnf 1882 Edinburgh. [NAS.SC70.1.218/366]

ANDERSON, GEORGE, at Medical Lake, Washington, 1899, son of Elizabeth Carnegy or Anderson in Little Brechin, Angus, who died 16 March 1898. [NAS.SH.5.5.1899]

ANDERSON, JAMES, from Johnstone, Dumfries-shire, formerly a surgeon with the East India Company, died in Jefferson County, Indiana, on 21 October 1819. [DGC:7.3.1820]

ANDERSON, JAMES A., architect in Detroit 1878.
[NAS.SC48.49.25.78/171]

ANDERSON, Mrs JOHN, late of 70 Tolbooth Street, Leith, died in
Salt Lake City, Utah, in 1874. [S#9583]

ANDERSON, JOHN WALLACE, in Salina, Kansas, son of
Thomas Anderson, a blacksmith in Fenwick, Ayrshire, who
died 19 October 1876. [NAS.SH.21.8.1896]

ANDERSON, JOHN, in Chicago, 1882. [NAS.PS3.17.70]

ANDERSON, JOHN, a tinsmith from Edinburgh, died in Kelly's
Mechanics Hotel, Kansas City, on 15 April 1883. [S#12,487]

ANDERSON, JOHN, born in 1870, son of Alexander Anderson gas
manager in West Wemyss, Fife, a store clerk in San
Barnardino, California, died there on 19 March 1893. [PJ,
6.5.1893]

ANDERSON, LAUCHLAN, son of Mrs Margaret Moncreiff or
Anderson in Fife, settled in Detroit. [Probate 1785 PCC]

ANDERSON, MAGGIE, or INKSTER, born in Scotland during
1870, daughter of Hannah Anderson, wife of John Inkster,
died in San Francisco in December 1897. [San Francisco
Call, 7.12.1897]

ANDERSON, PETER, from Earlston, Berwickshire, died in San
Francisco on 12 October 1877. [S#10,705]

ANDERSON, PORTER, died in Rushville, Schuyler County,
Illinois, cnf 7 November 1882 Edinburgh.
[NAS.SC70.1.218/356]

ANDERSON, ROBERT, died in San Francisco in February 1853.
[EEC#22421]

ANDERSON, or STRACHAN, SUSAN, from Backwynd, Forfar,
then at Central Park, Chicago, 1875.
[NAS.RS.Forfar.30.166]

ANDERSON, THOMAS, born 1795, son of George Anderson and Agnes Kerr in Inverkeillor, Angus, died in New Orleans on 1 August 1835. [Inverkeillor g/s]

ANDERSON, VIOLET ALEXANDRA, in Clymer, Oregon, great grand-daughter of Alexander Anderson and Isabel Noble who died in 1854. [NAS.SH.9.10.1891]

ANDERSON, WILLIAM, from Renfrewshire, died in Illinois on 20 November 1862. [S#2347]

ANDERSON, WILLIAM FERRIE GENTLE, from Glasgow, married Harriet Hopkins, third daughter of R.B. Mason in Chicago on 19 September 1872. [S#9108]

ANDERSON, WILLIAM LIVINGSTON, from Edinburgh, but in St Paul, Minnesota, married Lizzie, second daughter of William P. Townsend of New Brighton, Pittsburg, PA, there on 22 June 1871. [S#8720]

ANDERSON, ..., daughter of W. L. Anderson, was born in St Paul, Minnesota, on 11 June 1872. [S#9025]

ANDERSON, ..., daughter of W. L. Anderson, was born in St Paul, Minnesota, on 23 January 1876. [S#10,156]

ANDERSON, ..., son of George Anderson, was born in Emerson, Iowa, on 19 July 1878. [S#10,939]

ANDERSON, ..., son of John Anderson, was born in Dale, Indiana, on 23 January 1879. [S#11,097]

ANDERSON, ..., son of John Anderson, was born in Dale, Indiana, on 26 January 1883. [S#12,351]

ANNANDALE, ERNEST VICTOR, in Clifton, Graham County, Arizona, cnf Edinburgh 1899. [NAS.SC70.1.375/410]

ARMOUR, ANDREW, a joiner, married Mary Gilmour in Illinois during June 1864. [NRH/MRB]

ARMSTRONG, HELEN, youngest daughter of the late George Armstrong, from Dumfries-shire, married David Robertson, eldest son of John Robertson, joiner in Rigg of Gretna,

Dumfries-shire, at Fairfax Vicarage, Linn County, Iowa, on 28 September 1888. [AO: 19.10.1888]

ARMSTRONG, MARY, born 1813, widow of John Ritchie, foermerly a farmer in Birkshawhead, Kirkpatrick Fleming, Dumfries-shire, died in Foosland, Champaign County, Illinois, on 11 February 1895. [AO:22.3.1895]

ARMSTRONG, Colonel ROBERT, a farmer in Nemaha County, Kansas, son of Robert Armstrong a farmer in Thircoon, Canonbie, Dumfries-shire, 1876. [AO]

ARMSTRONG, WILLIAM, born 1857, son of John Armstrong, Caroline Park, Edinburgh, died at the residence of his uncle in Kansas on 8 June 1884. [S#12793]

ASHBRIDGE, J. K., died in New Orleans on 4 November 1874. [S#9784]

ASHTON, EDWARD, in California around 1857. [NAS.SH.2.2.1857]

ATKIN or TURNBULL, MARY, born in 1784, emigrated from Creca, Annan, Dumfries-shire, to America in 1813, died in West Union, Fayette County, Iowa, on 11 October 1876. [AO]

ATKINS, Mrs, and her two daughters, arrived in San Francisco on 4 December 1852 aboard the barque Mysore, Captain Battly, from Glasgow. [SFL#4/201]

AUCHMUTY, CATHERINE, daughter of John Auchmuty in Bowhouse, Wemyss, Fife, married George Hardie, son of James Hardie in Sheephousewells, Dunfermline, Fife, at Fowler, Fresno County, California, on 8 April 1891. [DJ]

AULD, JAMES, youngest son of Robert Auld in Buteland, Balerno, Midlothian, died in San Francisco on 27 August 1884. [S#12853]

AUSTIN, ROSE, arrived in San Francisco on 13 July 1851 on board the William, Captain Gellatly, from Glasgow. [SFL#1/175]

BAILLIE, ROBERT, from Edinburgh but in Detroit, married
Jeannie, youngest daughter of James Nelson from
Edinburgh, in Hamilton, Ontario, 18 March 1872. [S#8971]

BAIN, ANTHONY, born in Dundee, son of James Bain and
Elizabeth Ruglen, emigrated to British Columbia before
1870, settled in Port Ludlow, Washington Territory, died on
27 September 1885. [WSP]

BAIN, JANE ANN, from Forres, Morayshire, settled in Oquanka,
Illinois, before 1870. [NAS.SH.1.9.1870]

BAIN, WILLIAM E., son of Edward Bain in Greenlaw,
Berwickshire, settled in Cherokee Flats, California, before
1882.[NAS.SH.22.12.1882]

BAIRD, AGNES, born in Methil, Fife, wife of James Pringle a
painter from Dundee, died in Springfield, Missouri, on 19
March 1891. [FFP]

BAIRNSFATHER, ISABELLA CREAR, died in New Orleans on
11 September 1878. [S#10,984]

BALFOUR, THOMAS N., in Halsey Linn County, Oregon, 1892.
[NAS.RS.Kirkcaldy.27.43]

BALFOUR,........, son of Robert Balfour, was born in San Francisco
on 8 September 1882. [S#12,224]

BALLANTYNE, JAMES BURN, born in 1829, son of William
Ballantyne a teacher in Edinburgh, the assessor for Kinnly
County, Texas, died in Brackett, Texas, on 4 December
1877. [St Cuthbert's g/s, Edinburgh][S#10,760]; in Fort
Clark, Texas, 1871. [NAS.SH.1871]

BALLENTYNE, RICHARD W., born 1814, died at the Battle of the
Alamo, Texas, on 6 March 1836. [TSHA#28.0/534]

BALLINGALL, CHARLOTTE, daughter of Alexander Ballingall,
Burnmill, Leven, Fife, and widow of Alexander Sime, died
in Dubuque, Iowa, on 30 November 1878. [S#11,056]

BALLINGALL, JAMES, possibly from Perth, settled in San
Francisco before 1854. [NAS.SH.25.7.1854]

BALLINGALL, LAURENCE, settled in Missouri before 1854.
[NAS.SH.25.7.1854]

BANDEEN, BARBARA, from Alford, Aberdeenshire, settled in
Ohio in 1833, married William Coutts, settled in Red Oak, Cedar
County, Iowa, died in 1848. [ENES#1.252]

BANDEEN, JOHN, from Alford, Aberdeenshire, died in Red Oak
Grove, Cedar County, Iowa, on 16 January 1854.
[AJ:22.2.1854]

BANDEEN, RACHEL, from Alford, Aberdeenshire, settled in Ohio
by 1833, married William Coutts after 1848, settled in Red
Oak, Cedar County, Iowa. [ENES#1.252]

BARCLAY, PETER, in Hazlewood, Wisconsin, cnf 1876
Edinburgh. [NAS.SC70.1.178/140]

BARKER, J., arrived in San Francisco from Glasgow on board the
barque Madeira, Captain Douglas, on 9 November 1851.
[SFL#3/2]

BARLAND, THOMAS, son of John Barland in Stormontfield,
Perthshire, settled in Wisconsin before 1862.
[NAS.SH.10.1.1862]

BARNET, GEORGE, from Aberdeen, died in Lockport, Will
County, Illinois, on 5 January 1861. [AJ:8.5.1861]

BARNET, JOHN, 159 Newberry Avenue, Chicago, 1889.
[NAS.RS.Forfar.48.268]; cousin of Betty Barnet who died
14 March 1888 wife of James Rae a weaver in Forfar,
Angus. [NAS.SH.29.10.1889]

BARNET, LEWIS, born in Aberdeen during 1773, died in Lockport,
Illinois, during 1856. [AJ:12.11.1856]

BARR, THOMAS, a mine worker in Terre Haute, Indiana, cnf 1884
Edinburgh. [NAS.SC70.1.234/811]

BARRIE, ROBERT, son of John Barrie and Mary Findlay in
Newmilns, Ayrshire, settled in Blair, Michigan, before
1870.[NAS.SH.14.10.1870]

BARRIE, ROBERT, from Leith, married Jessie Robb, eldest
daughter of Walter Robb, Inveresk, Musselburgh, in Detroit
on 26 June 1871. [S#8724]

BARRIE, ...,daughter of Robert Barrie, was born in Detroit on 14
September 1872. [S#9107]

BARRON, JAMES STEINSON, born 1851, died in Los Angeles,
California, 1 May 1875. [S#9934]

BARTLEMORE, T., arrived in San Francisco on 13 July 1851 on
board the <u>William</u>, Captain Gellatly, from Glasgow.
[SFL#1/175]

BARTON, JOHN, from Dumfries-shire, died in Minneapolis,
Minnesota, on 7 February 1869. [AO]

BAYNE, THOMAS, son of William Bayne and Agnes Blair in
Doune, Stirlingshire, settled in Idaho before 1859.
[NAS.SH.27.4.1859]

BEATTIE, Mrs ELIZABETH T., born in Annan, Dumfries-shire,
during 1784, died in Chico, California, on 24 December
1869. [AO]

BEATTIE, JOHN, born in 1809, youngest son of Dr Beattie in
Insch, Aberdeenshire, died in Aurora, Wisconsin Territory,
on 28 March 1839.[AJ#4766]

BEATTIE, WILLIAM, born in 1843, son of James Beattie in
Benwells, Old Deer, a stonecutter who died in St Louis on
15 August 1876. [AJ:13.9.1876]

BECKTON, JEAN, widow of John McPherson of Easdale, Argyll,
died in Cherokee, Iowa, on 1 June 1885. [AO: 3.7.1885]

BEITH, JOHN, son of John Beith a merchant in Rothesay, settled in
San Francisco before 1877. [NAS.SH.9.3.1877]

BELL, CATHERINE, born 1817, wife of William Roy, died in New
Orleans on 27 May 1858. [Cupar g/s, Fife]

BELL, JAMES, eldest son of George Bell in Leith, married Dorcas,
second daughter of James Langton, Bruree, County
Limerick, in San Francisco on 3 June 1854. [EEC#22612]

BELL, JAMES, born in 1821, second son of John Bell a farmer in Torduff, a merchant in Victoria, Vancouver Island, died in San Francisco on 19 June 1862. [AO]

BELL, JOHN, a merchant in St Louis, Missouri, died on 30 March 1860. [NAS.CC8.8.inv.1861]

BELL, JOHN, born 1839, fifth son of Captain Thomas Bell, Annan, Dumfries-shire, died in Vallejo, California, 21 December 1894. [AO: 16.8.1895]

BELL, JOHN, born in Edinburgh on 7 March 1828 son of Thomas Bell and Jane Tait, settled in Sequim, Washington Territory, by 1856, died there in 1896. [WSP]

BELL, WILLIAM, born 1808, son of John Bell and Janet Davidson in Middlebie, Dumfries-shire, a merchant in New Orleans from 1830, died 30 November 1838. [Pennershaugh g/s, Dumfries-shire]

BELL, WILLIAM, son of Janet Jardine or Bell in Kirkcudbright, in San Francisco 1876. [NAS.SH.20.9.1876]

BENVIE, GEORGE WILLIAM RODNEY, born 26 March 1877, son of Reverend Andrew Benvie in Scone, Perthshire, settled in New Mexico. [F#4/253]

BERWICK, DAVID, born in 1829, son of David and Jean Berwick, in Chicago with his wife Margaret Chiene in 1876, died in Oakland, California, on 12 February 1896. [St Andrews, Fife, g/s][NAS.SH.17.5.1876]

BEVERIDGE, ROBERT, from Kirkcaldy, Fife, died in Red Wing, Minnesota, on 11 February 1883. [S#12,366]

BINNING, ..., daughter of William J. Binning, was born at 220 East 9th St., St Paul, Minnesota, on 10 February 1879. [S#11,110]

BIRRELL, ..., daughter of Robert Birrell from Methil, Fife, was born in Chester, Thayer County, Nebraska, on 21 October 1888. [FFP]

BISSET, HENRY, in Palmyra, Wisconson, 1887, nephew of Grace Bisset a millworker in Dunfermline, Fife, who died in July 1882. [NAS.SH.19.112.1887]

BISSET, PATRICK DUFF, born 1823, from Aberdeen, son of Patrick Duff Bisset, died in Liberty, Texas, on 20 June 1860. [AJ:28.11.1860]

BISSET, ROBERT, possibly from Glasgow, a coach painter in Gonzales, Texas. 1863. [NAS.SH.1863]

BISSET, WALTER SCOTT, son of Patrick Duff Bisset [1823-1860], died in Liberty, Texas, on 1 November 1860. [AJ:28.11.1860]

BLACK, ALEXANDER LESLIE, born 1813 in Forres, son of Charles Black and Ann Leslie, died in New Orleans on 9 October 1837. [AJ#4692]

BLACK, ALEXANDER, born 1844, third son of John Black of the General Post Office in Edinburgh, died in San Francisco on 10 February 1873. [S#9244]

BLACK, DAVID, fifth son of Reverend James Black in Penningham, Wigtonshire, died in New Orleans in May 1840. [W#56]

BLACK, GEORGE MOIR, in Detroit, Michigan, son of James Black, from Nairn, a merchant in Detroit who died there on 12 July 1879. [NAS.SH.15.4.1897]

BLACK, HUGH, an oil merchant in Wyoming, 1865. [NAS.RS.Paisley.1.165]

BLACK, JAMES, from Inverness, settled in Canada de la Janive near Bodega Bay, California, in 1820s. [SHR#153/141]

BLACK, JAMES, in Ottawa, Kansas, by 1899, brother of William Dalziel Black who died in Salsburgh, Shotts, Lanarkshire, 11 September 1895. [NAS.SH.25.7.1899]

BLACK, JAMES, jr., born 1871, son of James Black, grandson of William Brown [1807-1887] and Helen McMillan [1810-1872], died in Oakland, California, 21 June 1904. [St Peter's, Spittal, Aberdeen, g/s]

BLACK, JANE M., daughter of T. Black formerly of the 'Gauze' and the 'William Craig' in West Lothian, married J. P. Williams, in Singleton Place, Lake County, Indiana, on 21 September 1881. [S#11,936]

BLACK, Mrs MARY HOLDEN, wife of Alexander David Martin Black, Writer to the Signet in Edinburgh, died in Long Beach, California, cnf Edinburgh 1899. [NAS.SC70.1.380/559]

BLACKSTOCK, JOSEPH, born around 1817, son of Joseph Blackstock in Brickfield, Troqueer, Kirkcudbrightshire, died in Alton, Illinois, on 15 October 1856. [DGC;18.11.1865]

BLAIR, DAVID BOYLE, in San Francisco, married Leila Kirkham second daughter of General R.W.Kirkham of the US Army, Oakland, California, there on 22 August 1872. [S#9096]

BLAIR, JAMES SCOTT, in Detroit, 1878. [NAS.SH.28.5.1878]

BLAIR, ..., daughter of S.C.Blair, was born in Hoprig, Emmet County, Iowa, on 20 June 1884. [S#12791]

BLAKE, FRANCES MARSHALL, daughter of William Blake a builder from Edinburgh, died in Evansville, Illinois, 1869. [S#8095]

BLAKE, WILLIAM, born 1862, only child of Mrs Blake from Edinburgh, died in Evanstown, Cook County, Illinois, on 27 May 1879. [S#11,212]

BLUNTACH, JAMES, son of John Bluntach in Forres, Morayshire, settled in Hastings, Minnesota, by 1872. [NAS.SH.17.7.1872]

BLYTH, ROBERT, a farmer in Racine, Wisconsin, 1882, possibly from Crail, Fife. [NAS.SH.9.8.1772]

BOAG, ROBERT, a mason in Dundee, Illinois, by 1869, son of Robert and Jean Boag in Easter Levan, Innerkip, Renfrewshire. [NAS.SH.27.7.1869]

BOGLE, ROBERT, a merchant from Glasgow, died in New Orleans in February 1826. [EA]

BONE, WALTER, born in 1826, youngest son of David Bone in Kilpatrick Juxta, Dumfries-shire, died in Huntsville, Missouri, on 2 March 1878. [AO]

BONELLA, ANN, daughter of John Bonella and Margaret Fernie, died in Kansas on 19 September 1859. [Leuchars, Fife, g/s]

BONNAR, JOHN, a ships carpenter from Elie, Fife, drowned off Port Costa, near San Francisco, on 3 September 1884. [S#12859]

BONTHRON, ANDREW, born 1777 in Moonzie, Fife, son of Alexander Bonthron and Elspet Coit, died in New Orleans on 17 August 1813. [Moonzie g/s]

BONTINE, ROBERT, in Nuences County, Texas, 1879. [NAS.GD22.3/548]

BOOTH, JOHN SIM, in Kingston, Michigan, by 1899, son of John Booth, a mason in Aberdeen, and his wife Jean Park who died 11 December 1896. [NAS.SH.26.9.1899]

BORTHWICK, AGNES JANE, wife of Reverend John Gordon minister of the Western Avenue baptist Church, late of Leslie, Fife, died in Chicago on 5 February 1871. [S#8611]

BORTHWICK, CHARLES, born in 1840, son of James Borthwick and Mary Milne, died in San Francisco on 12 August 1881. [Arbroath Abbey g/s, Angus] [NAS.SH.27.3.1877]

BORTHWICK, DAVID, settled in Bute Valley, Nevada, died on 20 February 1873. [NAS.SH.27.3.1877]

BORTHWICK, WILLIAM, born in 1846, son of James Borthwick and Mary Milne, died in Berkeley, California, on 27 September 1921.[Arbroath Abbey g/s, Angus]

BOYD, JOHN, son of Alexander Boyd in Paisley, Renfrewshire, settled in Vandale, Minnesota, by 1883. [NAS.SH.6.11.1883]

BOYLE, JOHN, born 1839, eldest son of John Boyle, Bank Street, Glasgow, died in St Louis, Missouri, on 6 November 1870. [S#8532]

BRAND, JAMES W., second son of William Brand, Mylnefield, Dundee, died in San Francisco on 6 July 1875. [EC#28326]

BRANDER, ..., daughter of George L. Brander, manager of the Nevada Bank of San Francisco, was born in San Francisco on 30 March 1883. [S#12,412]

BRANDER, ..., son of George L. Brander, manager of the Nevada bank of San Francisco, was born in San Francisco on 27 October 1884. [S#12907]

BREADY, JAMES, emigrated via St Louis to Salt Lake City, Utah, in 1853. [StAUL:MS32]

BREMNER, ALEXANDER, in Bent County, California, cnf Edinburgh 1887. [NAS.SC70.1.258/135]

BREMNER, JAMES, born in Rhynie, Aberdeenshire, on 26 December 1831 son of John Bremner and Margaret Cran, married Abigail Clark Freeman in Chicago during 1845, settled in Iowa, died in Delta, Washington, 19 March 1887. [WSP]

BREMNER, JESSAMINE ANNE, married Frank Collinson in Lamar, Colorado, 1887, settled in the Big Bend country, south west Texas. [TSHA#19/0491]

BRERETON, R. M., former factor to the Duke of Sutherland, settled in Forest Grove, Oregon, by 1890. [NAS.NRAS0852]

BRINE, ROBERT, in San Francisco, 1870. [NAS.SH.29.12.1870]

BROAD, JOHN W., born in 1826, fifth son of Michael Broad and Helen Walker in Galashiels, died in Paris, Texas, on 28 January 1877. [Kirkhope g/s][S#10,486]

BRODIE, Mrs FLORA, wife of John Brodie, born in Aberdeen during 1831, died in San Francisco on 8 September 1873. [San Francisco Morning Call, 9.9.1873]

BRODIE, JAMES BUCHANAN, only son of William Brodie [1815-1881] and Helen Chisholm [1817-1886], died in Corvallis, Oregon, on 22 November 1915. [Dean g/s, Edinburgh]

BRODIE, JOHN NICHOLSON, from Kirriemuir, Angus, married Amy, youngest daughter of Asa Hicks a farmer at Bear Lake, Manistee County, Michigan, there on 4 August 1872. [S#9084]

BROOKES, MARION, wife of Alexander Craig, from Edinburgh, died in 23 Bissell Street, Chicago, on 6 February 1881. [S#11,736]

BROWN, ALEXANDER, born 1843, from Aberdeen, soldier of the 7th US Cavalry in 1876. [S]

BROWN, ALICE, eldest daughter of R. S. Brown, photographer, Brougham Street, Edinburgh, married James Watt Graham, son of R. B. Graham, painter in Edinburgh, in Chicago, Illinois, on 21 July 1882. [S#12,190]

BROWN, ANDREW, born in Fife 1789, a joiner, emigrated to America before 1830, 'lived in the Far West before making Natchez his home', died there 28 January 1871. [Natchez Courier]

BROWN, ..., daughter of George Mabbott Brown, was born in Nortonville, California, on 8 July 1884. [S#12810]

BROWN, DAVID, in California, cnf 1882 Edinburgh. [NAS.SC70.1.215/635]

BROWN, JAMES, born during 1833, son of John Brown a mason in Rashiebriggs, Lochmaben, Dumfries-shire, died in St Louis, Missouri, on 30 September 1859. [DGH:11.11.1859]

BROWN, Mrs MARGARET, born in St Mungo, Dumfries-shire, during 1808, married John Brown, emigrated to Wisconsin in 1840, died in Dekorra, Wisconsin, on 27 August 1870. [AO]

BROWN, P.M., architect, youngest son of Robert Brown a linen manufacturer in Edinburgh, married Jeannie Dawson Currie, daughter of Andrew Currie in Ladykirk, Berwickshire, in Denver, Colorado, on 21 December 1881. [S#12,010]

BROWN, WILLIAM, born on 25 March 1781 in Alyth, Perthshire, son of John Brown and Margaret Haldane, emigrated to Iowa in 1820, married Margaret Main, died in Keokuk, Iowa, on 22 September 1821. [FPF]

BROWN, WILLIAM, late of Ardnamuddle, Aberdeenshire, died in Brownsville, Illinois, on 1 July 1849. [AJ#5299]

BROWN, ..., son of P. M. Brown, an architect, was born in Denver, Colorado, on 5 November 1882. [S#12,281]

BRUCE, DANIEL, born 1823, fourth son of John Bruce in Grantown-on-Spey, Morayshire, died in Sacramento, California, on 18 August 1874. [S#9720]

BRUCE, LAWRENCE, son of Alexander Bruce a mason in Burrelton, Perthshire, settled in St Louis before 1866. [NAS.SH.5.7.1866]

BRUCE, THOMAS, born 1797, a laborer, with Mrs Bruce born 1797, and Miss Bruce born 1807, emigrated via Port Glasgow to New Orleans on the Elizabeth, master A. Grierson, to settle in Louisiana, arrived in New Orleans on 12 November 1827. [USNA.M259/7]

BRUCE, WILLIAM ANDREW, born in 1854, son of John Bruce [1825-1895] and Christian Ritchie [1829-1871], died in Harford, California, on 12 October 1896. [Monymusk, Aberdeenshire, g/s]

BRYCE, ANDREW CARTER, in Fargo, Dakota, cnf 1887 Edinburgh. [NAS.SC70.1.256]

BRYCE, THOMAS, in Saugamon County, Illinois, cnf 1886 Edinburgh. [NAS.SC70.1.247/898]

BUCHAN, WILLIAM, at Sturgeon Bay, Wisconsin, nephew of Charles Buchan, a farmer at Keyhead, St Fergus, Aberdeenshire, who died on 8 April 1868. [NAS.SH.11.12.1897]

BUCHANAN, DANIEL, born in Glasgow on 25 February 1820 son of John Buchanan and Martha Scott, married Mary Shaw in Glasgow on 3 January 1845, died in Ritzville, Washington, on 23 May 1903.[WSP]

BUICK, KIRKWOOD H., in Melville, North Dakota, cnf 1891
Edinburgh. [NAS.SC48.49.25.190/87]

BUIST, CATHERINE, daughter of John Buist a weaver in
Sinclairtown, Kirkcaldy, Fife, settled in Bronzton, Michigan,
by 1879.[NAS.SH.25.6.1879]

BUIST, ROBERT, born in 1845, eldest son of James Buist in
Rankeiller, Cupar, Fife, died in Missouri City, Clay County,
Missouri, on 7 May 1873. [EC#27661][S#9313]

BURN, ..., daughter of Lewis A. W. Burn, Chicago, was born in
Camden, NJ, on 7 February 1878. [S#10,795]

BURN, ..., son of Lewis A. Burn, was born in Chicago, Illinois, on
23 April 1879. [S#11,178]

BURNETT, ROBERT, a lighthouse keeper in North Unst, Shetland
Islands, later in Chicago, cnf Edinburgh 1900.
[NAS.SC70.1.389/530]

BURNS, or THOMSON, JEAN, daughter of William Burns in
Eglinton, Ayrshire, settled in Whiteside County, Illinois, by
1873. [NAS.SH.21.5.1873]

BURNSIDE, ROBERT, born 1783, arrived in USA on 28 September
1803, a teacher in New Orleans. [1812]

BUTLER, ..., daughter of R. J. Butler, was born in San Francisco on
11 June 1873. [S#9348]

CAIN, ALEXANDER LAIRD, second son of William Cain of
Carron, and nephew of George Geddes in Glasgow, died at
80 West 13th Street, Chicago on 16 December 1878.
[EC#29424]

CAIRNCROSS, JAMES, born in 1786, from Carnoustie, Angus,
licenced as a minister of the Original Secession Church on 9
May 1815, a minister in Birsay from 1818 to 1842,
emigrated to Wisconsin, died in Blandford on 23 November
1851. [AOSC#541]

CAIRNS, ROBERT, born in Glasgow during 1824, died in San
Francisco on 18 August 1873. [San Francisco Morning Call,
20.8.1873]

CALDERWOOD, JOHN, possibly from Bute, settled in Illinois before 1869. [NAS.SH.24.5.1869]

CAMERON, EWEN, born around 1811, a soldier of the Texan Army in 1836, fought at the Battle of Lipantlan in 1842, executed by the Mexicans in 1843. [TSHA#30.0/533]

CAMERON, HUGH, born on 8 October 1852, son of Hugh Cameron and Jean Fairlie, died in Omaha on 2 September 1916. [Greenock g/s, Renfrewshire]

CAMERON, JAMES, son of James Cameron a slater in Inverness, settled as a commission agent in Detroit before 1857. [NAS.SH.9.1.1857]

CAMERON, JANET, or DALZIEL, in Illinois, 1 October 1855.[NAS.SC371/59/13/142]

CAMPBELL, ANDREW YOUNG, possibly from Fife, settled at Lake Superior before 1864. [NAS.SH.16.8.1864]

CAMPBELL, ARCHIBALD, born 1823, son of Archibald Campbell and Margaret Watt, died in New Orleans on 5 October 1839. [Perth, Greyfriars, g/s]

CAMPBELL, CECILIA, Dalziel Park, died in New Orleans in 1854. [S#4.11.1854]

CAMPBELL, DANIEL, from Airdrie, Lanarkshire, drowned in Lake Erie on 23 July 1850. [NAS.CC8.8.inv.1851]

CAMPBELL, DANIEL, jr., Dundee, Kane County, Illinois, died 28 August 1860. [NAS.CC8.8.inv.1862]

CAMPBELL, DONALD, at Detroit, 1761. [BL.Add.MS21,647/11-14]

CAMPBELL, DUGALD, of Skerrington, died in New Orleans on 24 October 1827. [SM#57.818]

CAMPBELL, ELIZABETH, born 1810, daughter of David Campbell (1788-1848) and Mary Porter (1785-1868), died in New Orleans on 1 September 1838, [Buittle g/s, Kirkcudbrightshire]

CAMPBELL, GEORGE, from Glasgow, a banker in Piper City, Illinois, by 1882. [NAS.SH.28.12.1882]

CAMPBELL, JAMES, an army officer in New Orleans and Mobile 1764, Arkansas 1765, and in Illinois 1767. [NAS.NRAS#0631]

CAMPBELL, JAMES, late of Illinois now resident in New York, probate 20 February 1770 New York

CAMPBELL, JAMES, of Bellefontain, late Captain Lieutenant of the 34th Regiment, barrackmaster in Illinois, husband of Anna Maxwell, probate September 1770 New York.

CAMPBELL, JAMES, born in Skye, Inverness-shire, 1844, emigrated to Prince Edward Island in 1858, settled in San Francisco during 1870s, a builder. [OCGS: 38.1.45]

CAMPBELL, JOHN, son of Neill Campbell in Sunipole, Argyll, died in Monroe, Ouchita, Louisiana, in 1845. [DGH.15.1.1846]

CAMPBELL, ..., daughter of John Campbell jr, from Edinburgh, was born in Mapleton, Dakota, on 11 November 1877. [S#10,735]

CAMPBELL, LACHLAN, born in 1842, son of Duncan Campbell [1805-1872] and Ann McLeod [1803-1883], died in Galveston, Texas, on 11 October 1867. [Greenock g/s]

CAMPBELL, PETER, in St Louis, Missouri, cnf 1878 Edinburgh. [NAS.SC70.1.187/779]

CANDLISH, JAMES, from Kirkcudbright, married Mary Gordon Ritchie, daughter of John Ritchie, High Street, Kirkcudbright, in Eureka, Nevada, on 4 November 1882. [S#12,292]

CANDLISH, ..., daughter of James Candlish and his wife Mary Ritchie, from Kirkcudbright, was born in Eureka, Nevada, on 20 November 1883. [S#12,610]

CARGILL, DAVID, in New Orleans, died 10 February 1846. [NAS.SH]

CARLYLE, JOHN SMITH, born 1842 in Annan, Dumfries-shire, manager of the Annan Cooperative store, emigrated to Chicago in 1871, rancher in Beatrix, Nebraska, died in Chicago 13 April 1895. [AO: 3.5.1895]

CARMICHAEL, JAMES RUTHERFORD, married Mary Anne Peter, daughter of Thomas H. Peter from Kirkland, Fife, in Ocheydan Close, Iowa, on 5 July 1882. [S#12,199]

CARMICHAEL, WILLIAM, possibly from Edinburgh, settled in Worth Tuscola, Michigan, by 1870. [NAS.SH.28.11.1870]

CARMICHAEL, WILLIAM, in Elmira, Michigan, 1886, brother of Jane Carmichael in Edinburgh who died 29 April 1867. [NAS.SH.19.6.1886]

CARRICK, JAMES, born in Stirling, son of William Carrick and Margaret Gardiner, married Adelaida Segand from New Orleans, in Louisiana on 19 March 1797. [LGS]

CARRUTH, JAMES, son of William Carruth a farmer in Birkenhead, Renfrewshire, settled in Utah before 1864. [NAS,SH.2.2.1864]; a farmer from Houston, Renfrewshire, then in Utah, 1866. [NAS.SC58.59.27.76]

CARSON, ARCHIBALD, born in 1849, died in Newtown, Iowa, on 9 October 1908. [Auchenleck g/s, Ayrshire]

CARSON, JOHN, born in 1810, son of Robert Carson of the Commercial Inn, Kirkcudbright, died in New Orleans on 27 December 1837. [DGC.15.3.1837]

CARSWELL, JOHN, possibly from Paisley, Renfrewshire, settled in Barry Pike County, Illinois, before 1870. [NAS.SH.28.4.1870]

CARTER, CHARLES, of Galena, born 1823, son of David Carter in Aberdeen, died at his brother's house in Chicago on 14 July 1860. [AJ:1.8.1860]

CARTER, JAMES, son of David Carter a blacksmith in Aberdeen, educated at Marischal College, Aberdeen, from 1831 to 1835, graduated MA, a banker and merchant in St Louis and in Chicago. [MCA#2/478]

CARTER, ..., son of James Carter, was born in Galena, Illinois, on 28 August 1851. [AJ#5411]

CASWELL, MILES, possibly from Paisley, Renfrewshire, settled as a farmer in Union City, Michigan, by 1879. [NAS.SH.6.7.1879]

CAUTION, DAVID, born 1880, son of David Caution, from Bryson Road, Edinburgh, died in Chicago on 25 May 1883. [S#12,460]

CHALMERS, GEORGE, a house carpenter from Strichen, Aberdeenshire, died at Panama on his way from California to Alabama in March 1852.[AJ:7.7.1852]

CHALMERS, JAMES, a blacksmith and engineer from Maxwelltown, Kirkcudbrightshire, died in Pine River, Wisconsin, on 8 August 1856.[DGC:28.10.1856]

CHALMERS, JAMES, in San Bernardino, California, cnf 1882 Edinburgh. [NAS.SC70.1.211/931]

CHALMERS, JOHN, son of John Chalmers and Elizabeth Christie in Burntisland, Fife, at 2028 Morgan Street, St Louis, Missouri, in 1883.[NAS.B9.1.283-286] [NAS.SH.19.4.1883][NAS.RS.Burntisland.11.169]

CHALMERS, PETER, youngest son of Peter Chalmers, farmer in Plains, Auchtermuchty, Fife, died in Trio, Texas, on 25 April 1879. [S#11,190]

CHALMERS, WATSON, son of C. Chalmers and Janet Arnot, a printer in Chico, California by 1867. [NAS.SH.1.8.1867]

CHAPMAN, JOHN, possibly from Edinburgh, settled in Washington, Illinois, by 1880. [NAS.SH.10.3.1880]

CHAPPELL, ALEXANDER, a shoemaker from Kirkton of Skene, Aberdeenshire, died at Red Oak Grove, Cedar County, Iowa, on 31 August 1874.[AJ:30.9.1874]

CHAPPELL, JOHN, from Aberdeenshire, emigrated to New York in 1833, settled in Iowa. [ENES#252]

CHARLES, ALEXANDER S., born on 18 August 1845 in Stonehaven, Kincardineshire, married Mary Jane MacAvoy in Ferndale, Whatcom, Washington Territory, on 13 May 1874, died in Bellingham, Whatcom, in 1922. [WSP]

CHARLES, JANE, daughter of John Charles in Edinburgh, a former factor for the Hudson Bay Company, married William R. Ramage, in Central City, Colorado, in 1874. [S#9700]

CARMICHAEL, WILLIAM, in Elmira, Michigan, brother of Jane Carmichael in Edinburgh who died 29 April 1867. [NAS.SH.19.6.1885]

CHEVALIER, Mrs J. B., and her two children, arrived in San Francisco on 12 April 1851 aboard the <u>Queen of Sheba</u>, Captain Cadell, from Leith. [SFL#1/125]

CHIENE, HUGH L. P., son of Major Chiene in Helensburgh, married Florence Emily Sugden, fourth daughter of Henry Sugden, Broughton, Manchester, in Lemars, Iowa, on 10 November 1881. [S#11,974]

CHIENE, ..., son of Hugh P, Chiene, was born in Lemars, Iowa, on 6 October 1882.[S#12,260]

CHIENE, ..., son of Hugh P. Chiene, was born in Yankton, Dakota, on 24 October 1884. [S#12898]

CHISHOLM, DONALD, born 1853, died in Delnorte, California, 24 March 1917. [Clachan Comair g/s, Kerrow, Inverness-shire.]

CHISHOLM, PETER, born in 1845, son of Peter Chisholm [1809-1880] and Margaret Ross [1805-1905], died in San Francisco on 4 June 1876.[Bowmore, Islay, g/s]

CHRISTIE, ALICE JANE, eldest daughter of James Christie of the British Linen Bank in Dundee, and wife of D. H. Johnston late of East Wemyss, Fife, and Dundee, died in Scio, Oregon, on 31 August 1901. [FFP]

CHRISTIE, HELEN, from Aberdeen, married Robert Hendrie, in San Francisco on 29 September 1856. [AJ#5680]

CHRISTIE, JOHN, possibly from Fife, settled in Chicago before 1850. [NAS.SH.17.7.1850]

CHRISTIE, THOMAS BURNETT, born 1851, son of Major Napier T. Christie, died in Montserrat, San Diego, California, 19 December 1874. [S#9822]

CHRISTIE, WILLIAM, born 1823, eldest son of John Christie of the Royal Hotel, St Andrews, Fife, died in Minnesota Territory on 8 May 1852.[FJ#1018]

CHRISTIE, ..., daughter of James Marshall Christie, was born at Craigend Farm, Paullina, O'Brian County, Iowa, on 2 August 1883. [S#12,514]

CHRISTISON, ANN HAY, in Colorado, cnf 1892 Edinburgh. [NAS.SC70.1.306]

CLAPERTON, ALEXANDER, son of Thomas Claperton a cooper in Gorebridge, Midlothian, settled as a storekeeper in Empire City, Kansas, by 1879. [NAS.SH.6.10.1679]

CLARK, GEORGE, possibly from Edinburgh, a butcher in Detroit by 1879. [NAS.SH.19.12.1879]

CLARK, JAMES ALEXANDER, born on 4 May 1868, son of James Clark [1821-1881] and Jane MacArthur [1829-1893], died at Colorado Springs in August 1893. [Paisley, Woodside g/s]

CLARK, JOHN, born in 1758, arrived in America in 1790, a minister in St Louis, Missouri. [1812]

CLARK, MAUDE, eldest daughter of J. M. Clark of Greely, married John Gardner, professor of Botany at the State University of Colorado, in Greenly, Colorado, on 4 August 1891. [AO: 21.8.1891]

CLARK, SAMUEL, son of Reverend Samuel Clark the incumbent of St Paul's, Aberdeen, died in Madison on 16 October 1880. [AJ:18.10.1880]

CLARK, THOMAS W., a carpenter and builder, eldest son of George Clark in Annan, Dumfries-shire, married Ellen Gardner, eldest daughter of Captain Gardner, in San Francisco on 1 May 1858.[AO]

CLARK, WILLIAM BENNET, in Texas, cnf 1886 Edinburgh.
[NAS.SC70.1.247/923]

CLARK, ..., twin sons of James Clark, were born in Kinglay, Iowa,
on 28 November 1885. [AO:25.12.1885]

CLEGHORN JAMES, born in Cupar, Fife, in 1833, master of the J.
P. Taylor, died in Chicago 5 December 1868. [S#7930]

CLERK, ..., daughter of Simon Clark, born at Walla Walla,
Washington Territory, on 11 November 1890. [AO:
8.12.1890]

CLERIHEW, ALEXANDER, granite merchant, Denhead, Kintore,
Aberdeenshire, then in Washington, 1902.
[NAS.RS.Kintore.8.92]

CLERIHEW, GEORGE MAURICE ALEXANDER, in Nebraska
by 1892, heir to Francis Clerihew a builder in Aberdeen who
died 18 December 1839. [NAS.SH.16.6.1892]

CLIBBORN, Mrs MARIA, born 1844, daughter of William George
Menzies Clibborn late paymaster of the 4th Regiment of
Foot, wife of Samuel M. Whittetsey, died at Pueblo,
Colorado, on 19 August 1877. [S#10,657]

CLINK, ANN, born in Dundee on 12 May 1833, daughter of Robert
Clink and Ann Stuart, married George Small Kiddie in
Dundee during 1860, emigrated to Victoria, British
Columbia, by 1864, settled in Washington Territory by 1869,
died in Seattle on 28 June 1910. [WSP]

CLOW, ROBERT, in Oregon Precinct, Illinois, cnf 1874
Edinburgh. [NAS.SC70.1.167/645]

CLUNAS, JAMES, born 1809, formerly in New Orleans, died in
Nairn 2 January 1888. [Wardlaw g/s, Inverness]

CLUNAS, JOHN, eldest son of Alexander Clunas, 3 South Howard
Place, Edinburgh, late in Nairn, died in Chicago on 29
December 1874. [S#9828]

COATES, MARY, daughter of William Coates in Townhead of
Greenlaw, Kirkcudbrightshire, married Robert Kirkpatrick,

in Whitepigeon, St Joseph's County, Michigan, on 20 July 1857. [DGC:21.8.1857]

COBURN, JAMES M., a banker in Kansas City, later founder of the Hansford Land and Cattle Company in 1880s. [TSHA.13.0/551]

COCKAYNE, FRANCIS HENRY, in Placer County, California, cnf 1898 Edinburgh. [NAS.SC70.1.365/924]

COCHRANE, ALEXANDER, born in 1855, son of James Cochrane and Jane Gemmel, died in California on 6 December 1891. [Balmaghie g/s, Kirkcudbrightshire]

COCKBURN, THOMAS, a butcher in Litchfield, Illinois, who died 22 January 1868, father of Agnes, Isabella and Mary. [NAS.SH.24.11.1890]

COLLIER, JAMES CURRIE, in Dubuque, Iowa, son of Robert Hutchison Collier, company manager there, who died 19 March 1896. [NAS.SH.4.1.1899]

COLQUHOUN, JAMES, brother of Peter Colquhoun a grocer in Edinburgh, died in Belvoir, Douglas County, Kansas, on 3 November 1879.[EC#29695][S#11,347]

COLQUHOUN, LUDOVIC, of Luss, died in Pleasant City, Atascoso City, San Antonio, Texas, on 9 March 1878. [EC#29176]

COLTART, SETH, born in 1809 son of James Coltart and Marion ..., died in California on 29 October 1851. [Buittle g/s, Kirkcudbrightshire]

COLVIN, WALTER, born 1850, eldest daugher of Rev. W. L. Colvin in Cramond, Midlothian, died in Glass Valley, Nevada, 16 Nov. 1872. [S#9167]

CONLEY, WILLIAM, born in 1845, died in Carson City, Nevada, on 9 January 1898. [Parton g/s]

CONNELL, AGNES, daughter of P. Connell a clothier in Hawick, Roxburghshire, married Leonard Luther, in Oakland, California, on 15 November 1877. [S#10,807]

CONNELL, JAMES ARTHUR, in Colorado Springs, son of Arthur Connell, a merchant in Glasgow, and his wife Jane Carrick who died 27 August 1896. [NAS.SH.28.10.1896]

COOPER, JAMES, born 25 December 1810 in Janetstown, Caithness, son of Alexander Cooper and Barbara Henderson, emigrated from Scotland to San Francisco around 1844, married Sarah Flint [1822-1886] in 1846, died in California on 6 September 1857. [FCP#36][Latheron g/s, Caithness]

COOPER, JAMES, from Aberdeenshire, emigrated to Poweshiek County, Iowa, in 1873. [ENES#1.253]

COOPER, ..., son of William Cooper, was born in Kansas on 16 June 1873. [S#9352]; died in Kansas on 30 August 1873. [S#9412]

COOPER, ..., son of William Cooper, was born at Neostro Falls, Kansas, on 17 July 1875. [S#10003]

COPELAND, DAVID, born in Scotland about 1860, died in San Francisco on 30 April 1887. [San Francisco Call, 3.5.1887]

CORBET, JOHN, a mariner in New Orleans, cnf 1882 Edinburgh. [NAS.SC70.1.214/163]

CORMACK, DONALD ANGUS, son of George Cormack and Margaret Cormack, died in South Dakota during July 1901. [Anwoth g/s, Kirkcudbrightshire]

CORNILLON, CHARLES, son of H.W.Cornillon, Solicitor to the Supreme Court of Scotland, died in Emmetsburg, Iowa, on 20 March 1882.[S#12,078]

COSKRY, MARY, born 1817, daughter of David Coskry in Leith, wife of Richard Petrie, from Elgin, Morayshire, died in Kansas on 1877. [S#10,500]

COUL, JOHN, born in 1821, son of John Coul and Ann Bissett, died in Windsor, California, on 3 December 1878. [Leuchars, Fife,g/s]

COULTER, JAMES, arrived in San Francisco in January 1850, married Margaret Duke, died around 1907. [FCP#39]

COULTHARD, Mrs MARGARET, wife of Captain William
Coulthard, both from Ruthwell, Dumfries-shire, died in
Aurora, Illinois, on 24 June 1872. [AO]

COUSIN, WILLIAM, a farmer in American Park City, Utah
County, Utah, 1876. [NAS.RS.Dysart.5.278]

COUSLAND, JOHN, youngest son of John Cousland a merchant in
Haddington, East Lothian, died at Indian Creek, Missouri, on
22 October 1873. [S#9454]

COUTTS, ADAM, born in 1817, from Oldtown Croft, Insch,
Aberdeenshire, died in Pleasant Township, Iowa, on 4 June
1875. [AJ:14.7.1875]

COUTTS, ELIZABETH, wife of Robert Pirie from Keig,
Aberdeenshire, died in Red Oak Grove, Cedar County, Iowa,
on 29 May 1853.[AJ:19.10.1853]

COUTTS, JAMES S., born in Arbroath, Angus, on 2 April 1847,
died in San Francisco on 4 June 1911, husband of Mary Ann
Coutts.[San Francisco Bulletin, 5.6.1911]

COUTTS, R. G., a stone mason from Insch, Aberdeenshire, settled in
Poweshiek County, Iowa, in 1874. [ENES#1.253]

COUTTS, WILLIAM, emigrated from Aberdeenshire to Ohio in
1834, settled in Red Oak township, Cedar County, Iowa, in
1837.[ENES#1.252]

COWAN, ANN JANE HAFFIE, was born in San Francisco,
California, on 16 May 1863 daughter of Hugh David Cowan,
a shipmaster, and Elizabeth Hetherington. [GRH#159]

COWAN, FRANCIS, in San Francisco, died 12 January 1852, cnf
1853 Edinburgh.[NAS.SC70.1.79]

COWAN, ROBERT, died in San Francisco in February 1853.
[EEC#22421]

COWAN, THOMAS, died in San Francisco on 12 January
1852.[NAS.CC8/8/inv.1853]

COWIE, ANDREW, born 1828, son of Andrew Cowie (1793-1857) and Marjory Macdonald (1797-1883), died in New Orleans in September 1854. [Inverness Chapel Yard g/s]

COWIE, JAMES, from Edinburgh, an artist in Colorado Springs, cnf 1896 Edinburgh. [NAS.SC70.1.348]

COWIE, JOHN REID, son of Alexander Cowie a surgeon in Aberdeen, settled in Indianapolis by 1883.
[NAS.SH.20.3.1833]

CRABBIE, WILLIAM JAMES, in Minneapolis, Minnesota, son of James Reid Crabbie who died in La Crosse, Wisconsin, on 14 November 1868. [NAS.SH.27.3.1896]

CRAIG, JAMES, born in 1818, son of D. Craig and M. Mather, died in Pueblo County, Colorado Territory, on 18 July 1860. [Eaglesham g/s, Renfrewshire]

CRAIG, JAMES ARTHUR, son of James Craig and Anne Turnbull in Glasgow, died in Chicago on 16 May 1881.
[NAS.SH.30.9.1881]

CRAIG, PETER, born in Coldingham, Berwickshire, in 1820, died in San Francisco on 27 July 1881. [San Francisco Morning Call, 31.7.1881]

CRAIGIE, ..., HBC trader, fortmaster at Fort Walla Walla on the Oregon Trail 1840s, 1850s. [HBRS]

CRAIGIE, WILLIAM, in Helena, Montana, cnf 1893 Edinburgh.
[NAS.SC70.1.316/603]

CRAM, WILLIAM FREDERICK, son of G. C. Cram and Agnes Jackson, settled in Oregon, Illinois, by 1878.
[NAS.SH.23.10.1878]

CRAWFORD, DAVID INGLIS, born in 1854, third son of William Crawford, 16 Montgomerie Street, Ardrossan, Ayrshire, died in Portland, Oregon, 1877.[EC#29092]

CRAWFORD, HUGH, son of William Crawford, settled in Chicago by 1867.[NAS.SH.15.2.1867]

CRAWFORD, JAMES, from Ladystoun, Strathallan, Perthshire, died in Aurora, Indiana, on 4 November 1871. [S#8833]

CRAWFORD, JOHN, born in Ayrshire during 1794, a weaver, emigrated to America during 1818, arrived in St Louis by 1819, settled in Howard County, Missouri, died on 14 January 1878, buried in Middletown Cemetery. [IGS]

CRAWFORD, JOHN, British consul in New Orleans in 1838. [NAS.GD121.82/105]

CRAWFORD, THOMAS, born 1835, a machinist, son-in-law of Daniel Wilson, 5 Saunders Street, Edinburgh, died in Detroit, Michigan, on 25 October 1877. [S#10,709]

CRAWFORD, Miss ...., arrived in San Francisco on 22 February 1852 on board the Hindustan, Captain Pook, from Glasgow. [SFL#3/83]

CREE, JAMES, in New Mexico, cnf 1891 Edinburgh. [NAS.SC70.1.298]

CRICHTON, JOHN, possibly from Fife, a stock-keeper in Iowanna, Illinois, by 1882. [NAS.SH.13.10.1882]

CROOKS, JESSIE DUNCAN, third daughter of Thomas crooks a merchant in Glasgow, married Alfred Hill, in Gardner, Illinois, on 24 November 1870. [S#8540]

CROOKS, RAMSAY, born in Greenock, Renfrewshire, on 28 January 1786, a fur trader and explorer in Oregon and Washington, later a merchant and director of an insurance company in New York, married Emilie Maison in St Louis during 1825, died in New York on 6 January 1859. [ANY.2.150]

CROOKSTON, WILLIAM LAW, son of Thomas Crookston a clerk in Brewsterford, settled in Iowa by 1857. [NAS.SH.24.9.1857]

CROWE, ALEXANDER, born 1840, son of David Crowe in Scrometin, Berwick-on-Tweed, died in Indianapolis on 26 August 1872. [S#9084]

CRUICKSHANK, ALEXANDER, born in 1827, from Aberdeen, died in Little Rock, Arkansas, in 1864. [AJ:16.11.1864]

CUMMING, ALEXANDER BEATTIE, brother of Robert Cumming a bookseller in Doune, Perthshire, settled in De Witt, Iowa, by 1890. [NAS.SH.2.7.1890]

CUNNINGHAM, GEORGE, fifth son of James Cunningham in Bonnington, Edinburgh, died in North Grove, Cass County, Illinois, on 25 May 1869. [S#8074]

CUNNINGHAM, JAMES, born in Govan, Glasgow, during 1801, emigrated to America in 1823, a ship owner and mechanical engineer in New York, Boston and San Francisco, died in Irvington on Hudson 28 April 1870 [ANY.292]

CUNNINGHAM, JAMES, possibly from Edinburgh, settled in California by 1859. [NAS.SH.2.3.1859]

CUNNINGHAM, MARGARET, daughter of Andrew Cunningham of Allandale, married A. S. Dodds MD, of Menard County, in Allandale, Cass County, Illinois, on 10 September 1863. [S#2595]

CURRIE, GEORGE, second son of William Currie in Greenland, Roxburghshire, died in New Orleans in January 1829. [EEC#18655]

CURRIE, JEANNIE DAWSON, daughter of Andrew Currie in Ladykirk, Berwickshire, married P.M.Brown, an architect from Edinburgh, youngest son of Robert Brown in Edinburgh, in Denver, Colorado, on 21 December 1881. [S#12,010]

CURTIS, ..., daughter of Charles W. Curtis, was born in Oaklands, Sedalia, California, on 19 December 1881. [EC#30356]

CUTHBERT, JANET, in Grand Rapids, Michigan, cnf 1874 Edinburgh. [NAS.SC70.1.169/93]

DALGITY, JAMES, in Carneiro, Kansas, 1886, son of Ann Nicoll or Dalgity or Grant in Kirriemuir, Angus, who died 8 September 1884. [NAS.SH.11.6.1884]

DALGITY, or CAMPBELL, JANE, from Caldhame, Forfar, then in Soloman City, Kansas, 1871. [NAS.RS.Forfar.26.163]

DALGLEISH, CATHERINE CRAIG, daughter of Adam Dalgleish [1794-1855]and Martha Cameron [1808-1858], settled in San Francisco. [Tulliallan g/s, Perthshire]

DALGLEISH, WILLIAM, in Hutton, Olin, Jones County, Iowa, cnf Edinburgh 1899. [NAS.SC70.1.379/666]

DALL, WILLIAM, born in 1797, died in Racine, Wisconsin, on 24 May 1877. [Newburgh g/s, Fife]

DALZIEL, GEORGE D., eldest son of John Dalziel, WS, Edinburgh, died at Yosemite, California, on 20 October 1884. [S#12881]

DARLING, ANDREW, an engraver in Chicago, [late of Thomas Nelson and Sons, Publishers in Edinburgh], married Maggie Barnes of Memphis, Tennessee, there on 24 April 1873. [EC#27647]

DARLING, J. G., an accountant with the Canadian Bank of Commerce in Chicago, married Lizzie M. Switzer, daughter of T. Switzer in Toronto, in Walkerton, Canada, on 14 September 1875. [S#10047]

DAVIDSON, AGNES, third daughter of William Davidson a merchant in Wick, Caithness, married E. S. Babcock a merchant, in Madison, Indiana, on 28 May 1844. [AJ#5044][EEC#21080]

DAVIDSON, ANNIE, in Appleton City, Missouri, grand-daughter of John Davidson a merchant in Aberdeen who died 2 December 1853. [NAS.SH.19.9.1890]

DAVIDSON, DAVID WILLIAM, a merchant in Omaha, Nebraska, cnf 1887 Edinburgh.[NAS.SC70.1.255]

DAVIDSON, DONALD, born in 1812, late from Columbo, Ceylon, died in San Francisco on 29 January 1875. [EC#28216]

DAVIDSON, HUGH, from Annan, Dumfries-shire, son of Captain H. Davidson, Secretary of the Caledonian Club of San Francisco, 1868. [AO]

DAVIDSON, HUGH, married Mary F. Metcalf in San Francisco on 3 October 1885. [AO:6.11.1885]

DAVIDSON, HUGH, fifth son of Captain Hugh Davidson in Annan, Dumfries-shire, died in San Francisco on 11 November 1891. [AO:27.11.1891]

DAVIDSON, ISABELLA, second daughter of William Davidson in Wick, Caithness, married John Ingle from Evansville, in Madison, Indiana, on 29 November 1842. [AJ#4958]

DAVIDSON, JAMES, son of James Davidson a stonecutter in Montrose, Angus, settled in Vancouver, Washington Territory, by 1864.[NAS.SH.30.12.1864]

DAVIDSON, JAMES, a carpenter in Portland, Oregon, son of Roderick Davidson, a farmer in Inverness, who died 13 January 1888. [NAS.SH.19.9.1888]

DAVIDSON, JOHN H., a merchant in San Francisco, married Mary Rae, youngest daughter of Andrew Rae a farmer in Broom, parish of Cummertrees, Dumfries-shire, there on 11 August 1863. [AO]

DAVIDSON, JOHN, born 1815, son of James Davidson a farmer in Hindlee, Roxburghshire, died in Chillicoth, Illinois, on 5 July 1879. [S#11,242]

DAVIDSON, MARY, born 1853, wife of James Davidson, died in Maywood, Mason County, Indiana, on 4 August 1887. [AO: 19.8.1887]

DAVIDSON, MARY JANE, born 1875, daughter of John Davidson and grand-daughter of the late John Davidson, died in Huron City, Michigan, 11 January 1893. [AO:3.3.1893]

DAVIDSON, NANCY WOODBURN, in Appleton City, Missouri, grand-daughter of John Davidson a merchant in Aberdeen who died 2 December 1853. [NAS.SH.19.9.1890]

DAVIDSON, ROBERT T., born 1793, died in Texas on 30 June 1838. [Anwoth g/s, Kirkcudbrightshire]

DAVIDSON, WILLIAM, MD, in Madison, Indiana, son of William Davidson a fish curer in Wick, Caithness, in 1863, 1864.[NAS.SC20.34.46.267-271] [NAS.SH.7.1.1864][NAS.RS27.83.275]

DAVIDSON, WILLIAM, a merchant in San Francisco, married Jane Crosbie, daughter of Theodore Crosbie classics master at Annan Academy, Dumfries-shire, in Annan on 30 July 1872. [AO][S#9057]

DAVIDSON, WILLIAM, a merchant, fourth son of Captain Hugh Davidson, died in San Francisco on 10 January 1879. [AO: 2.1.1880]

DAVIDSON, WILLIAM BRUCE, in Chicago, brother of Janet Bruce Davidson in Rattray, Perthshire, who died on 2 August 1897. [NAS.SH.17.11.1897]

DAVIDSON, ..., daughter of William Davidson, was born in San Francisco on 18 June 1875. [AO]

DAVIE, ALEXANDER, from Chapel of Garioch, Aberdeenshire, emigrated to Ohio, settled in Ashland County, married Isobel Duffus, from Insch, Aberdeenshire, settled in Poweshiek County, Iowa, in 1866.[ENES#1.253]

DAWSON, ELIZABETH HARRIETTE, born in 1853, daughter of William Dawson and Harriette Clark, wife of A. Tough, died in Chicago 15 February 1890. [East Preston Street cemetery, Edinburgh]

DEAN, ..., son of Robert Dean, late of 40 Reid Terrace, Edinburgh, was born in Tecumseh, Michigan, on 11 November 1867. [S#7602]

DEVLIN, H., arrived in San Francisco on 13 July 1851 on board the William, Captain Gellatly, from Glasgow. [SFL#1/175]

DEVLIN, WILLIAM, infant son of Henry Francis Devlin, died in South Valleys, California, in 1882. [S#12,210]

DEWAR, JAMES, son of James Dewar in Strathkinness, Fife, a patternmaker in Chicago, 1865. [NAS.SH.4.10.1865]

DEWAR, WILLIAM, from Edinburgh, married Margaret F. Barron widow of Henry Milward of Chicago, in Chicago on 16 May 1884. [S#12,734]

DICK, FANNIE MUSSELMAN, daughter of Thomas P. Dick of Rosebank, married L. W. Ward, at Rosebank, Clarksview, Red River, Texas, on 1 November 1876. [S#10,423]

DICK, JAMES BROWNLEE, born in Carluke, Lanarkshire, on 23 March 1835, son of James Dick and Margaret Brownlee, married Margaret Dewar on 21 September 1858, died in Sequim, Washington Territory, on 9 June 1898. [WSP]

DICK, THOMAS, a farmer in Indiana by 1836. [NAS.SH.6.6.1836]

DICK, WILLIAM, born in Scotland during 1817, died in San Francisco on 17 December 1868. [Daily Alta California, 18.12.1868]

DICKIE, JOHN, born in Scotland during 1831, died in San Francisco on 25 February 1886. [San Francisco Morning Call, 2.3.1886]

DICKISON, GEORGE, son of Alexander Dickison in Edinburgh, a joiner in Mound City, Illinois, by 1864. [NAS.SH.28.4.1864]

DICKSON, ABRAHAM, son of Reverend Jacob Dickson minister of Mousewald, Dumfries-shire, settled in Republican township, Jefferson County, Indiana, by 1825. [NAS.RD5.298.296]

DICKSON, JAMES, youngest son of John Dickson, Church Street, Tranent, East Lothian, married Harriet Euphemia Horsburgh, fifth daughter of William Horsburgh, South Queensferry, West Lothian, in Chicago on 28 July 1883. [S#12,510]

DICKSON, JANE LEVINA, infant daughter of Alexander and Lucy Dickson, died in Farmington, Minnesota, on 14 July 1868. [AO]

DICKSON, PETER, in Sanborn, Dakota, 1883. [NAS.SH.1.10.1883]

DICKSON, RICHARD LOWTHIAN, son of Reverend Jacob Dickson minister of Mousewald, Dumfries-shire, settled in

Republican township, Jefferson County, Indiana, by 1825.
[NAS.RD5.298.296]

DINNELL, GEORGE, born in 1808, Bishopton, Whithorn,
Wigtownshire, settled in Brownstone, Michigan, during
1855. [DGC:8.3.1859]

DOBIE, Mrs AGNES, born 1816, a widow from Dunfermline, Fife,
died in Kansas City, Missouri, on 27 December 1898. [DJ]

DOBIE, HELEN ANN, daughter of William Cowan Dobie and
Agnes Matthewson in Dunfermline, Fife, married Cyril
Randolph Smyth, in Raton, New Mexico, on 2 April 1891.
[DJ]

DOBIE, ISABELLA, daughter of William Dobie from Lockerbie,
Dumfries-shire, married Thomas Murdoch in Chicago on 30
March 1866. [AO]

DOBIE, JANE, daughter of William Cowan Dobie and Agnes
Matthewson in Dunfermline, Fife, married J. S. White, in
Berkeley, California, on 20 May 1890. [DJ]

DOBIE, JESSIE MATTHEWSON, daughter of William Cowan
Dobie and Agnes Matthewson in Dunfermline, Fife, married
Hugh J. Woods from Belfast, Ireland, in Raton, New
Mexico, on 18 December 1888, later settled in Kansas City,
Missouri. [DJ]

DOBIE, MARY, daughter of William Dobie from Lockerbie,
Dumfries-shire, married John Lyon from Paris, Canada
West, in Chicago on 30 March 1866. [AO]

DOBSON, GEORGE, from Edinburgh, a Captain of the Confederate
States Army, died in Houston, Texas, on 10 January 1870.
[S#8276]

DOBSON, JOHN, born in 1817, from Sanquhar, Dumfries-shire,
died in San Francisco on 30 December 1859.
[DGC:13.3.1860]

DOBSON, WILLIAM, born 16 March 1867 in Heathbank, Rattray,
Perthshire, son of David Dobson and Isabella Will, married
Isabella Walker in Detroit 20 November 1889, naturalised in

Detroit, Wayne County, Michigan, Recorder's Court 20 July 1896. [Court Records]

DODDS, MACRAE, in Calistoga, California, son of John Dodds, a farmer in Meikleriggs deceased and Mary Smith who died 16 February 1868. [NAS.SH.19.2.1885]

DODDS, THOMAS, second son of William Dodds in Annan, Dumfries-shire, died on Smith's Ranch, Place County, Colorado, on 20 December 1880. [AO:4.2.1881]

DODDS, WILLIAM, for 50 years a cabinetmaker with Mr Sandeman cabinetmaker in Edinburgh, died in Unadilla, Livingston County, Michigan, in November 1881. [S#12,015]

DOIG, BARBARA S., third daughter of A. Doig, Hilton of Fearn, Angus, married Boyd Emery Black, in Villsca, Iowa, on 6 September 1877. [S#10,668]

DOIG, THOMAS, son of James Doig a manufacturer in Dundee, an accountant of the Eastern Bank in Anstruther, Fife, died in Pescadera, Santa Cruz County, California, 27 November 1863. [EFR]

DOLLAR, JAMES, born during June 1849 in Grahamston, Stirlingshire, son of William Dollar and Mary Melville, died in San Rafael, California, in March 1898. [Falkirk g/s]

DONALDSON, ANN, widow of ... Alston, settled in Chicago before 1867.[NAS.SH.15.2.1867]

DOUGALL, ROBERT KIRKLAND, born in 1863, son of William Dougall and Mary Kirkland, died in Timberline, Cabaline, Montana, on 21 September 1890. [Cambusnethan g/s, Lanarkshire]

DOUGLAS, DAVID, born 1798 in Scone, Perthshire, botanist in California, Oregon and Washington, 1823 to 1832, died in Hawaii 1834. [Scone g/s]

DOUGLAS, JOHN, born in 1830, son of Archibald Douglas and Helen Bain, died in California on 18 March 1889. [Sannox g/s, Bute]

DOUGLAS, JOHN, from Urray, Ross-shire, settled in California, cnf 1891 Edinburgh. [NAS.SC70.1.301/309]

DOUGLAS, MARGARET, youngest daughter of Captain W. D. Douglas, The Croft, Annan, Dumfries-shire, married Samuel Martin Irvine of Dayville, in Dalles, Oregon, on 8 June 1896. [AO: 28.6.1896]

DOUGLAS, TOM, born in Perth during 1850, died in 1906. [Blewett Pass Cemetery, Chelan County, Washington]

DOUGLAS, WILLIAM JOHN, eldest son of Captain W. Douglas, The Croft, Annan, Dumfries-shire, and husband of Florence Dales Douglas, was drowned off Cape St Elias, Alaska, on 14 April 1895. [AO: 7.6.1895]

DOW, ANDREW, born in 1850, eldest son of Charles Dow the Sheriff Officer of Dunfermline, Fife, died in San Francisco, on 28 May 1888. [DJ]

DOW, ROBERT, born 26 May 1753, son of Reverend Robert Dow (1707-1787) and Janet Adie, a physician from Greenock, later in New Orleans 1843. [NAS.SH][F#3.79]

DOWNIE, CHARLES, a sheepman, settled in Terrell County, Texas, in 1881. [TSHA#32/0443]

DREW, JAMES, in Bingham, Idaho, 1889, cousin of James Drew, a laborer in Stewarton, who died 4 December 1888. [NAS.SH.1889]

DREW, WILLIAM CARFRAE, in Denver, Colorado, cnf 1894 Edinburgh. [NAS.SC70.1.329]

DRUMMOND, THOMAS, from Perthshire, a botanist in Texas 1833 to 1835, died in Havana

DUCAT, ..., daughter of Lawrence Leith Ducat late of the 92nd Gordon Highlanders, was born on Sicily Island, Louisiana, on 2 June 1878. [S#10,904]

DUFF, JAMES, from Kingoldrum, Angus, then in Denver, Colorado, 1884. [NAS.SC48.49.25.84/194]

DUFF, GEORGE, born 1836, third son of George Duff of the Commercial Hotel, Largo, Fife, died in San Francisco on 30 December 1876. [S#10,461]

DUFF, JAMES, in Denver, President of the Colorado Elevator and Warehouse Company, 1880. [NAS.GD255.box6]

DUFF, MAGGIE H., youngest daughter of James Duff manager of the Colorado Mortgage and Investment Company, died in Denver, Colorado, on 13 October 1878. [S#10,995]

DUFFUS, ALEXANDER, a farmer from Insch, Aberdeenshire, emigrated with his wife and family to Poweshiek County, Iowa, in 1854. [ENES#1.253]

DUFFUS, GEORGE, a farmer from Insch, Aberdeenshire, emigrated to Iowa in 1871, settled in Poweshiek. [ENES#1.253]

DUFFUS, JAMES, a farmer from Insch, Aberdeenshire, emigrated with his wife and family to Poweshiek County, Iowa, in 1854. [ENES#1.253]

DUGUID, ALEXANDER, in Berlin, Wisconsin, by 1896, son of Alexander Duguid, a paving cutter in Auchmill who died 11 September 1895. [NAS.SH.31.3.1896]

DUN, ROBERT PAIRMAN, MD, born 1819, son of Reverend William Dun in Edinburgh, died in Racine, Wisconsin, on 7 October 1882. [S#12,274]

DUNCAN, DAVID GRIEVE, born 1829 in Edinburgh, son of Reverend Dr Alexander Duncan, died in New Orleans, Louisiana, on 1 December 1879. [S#11,416]

DUNCAN or HAMILTON, JANE, in New Orleans, 1834. [NAS.SC37.59.8/69]

DUNCAN, MARGARET MITCHELL, infant daughter of William and Isabella Duncan, died in Princeton, Indiana, on 7 September 1877. [S#10,666]

DUNCAN, THOMAS, son of George Duncan a mason in Newhaven, Edinburgh, was drowned in the wreck of the

Excelsior in Thunder Bay on 15 October 1872 between Milwaukee and Buffalo. [S#9169]

DUNCAN, ..., daughter of William Duncan, was born in Princeton, Indiana, on 22 November 1876.[S#10,424]

DUNN, JOHN RITCHIE, in San Francisco, cnf 1881 Edinburgh. [NAS.SC70.1.210/781]

DUNN, ROBERT, born in Glasgow on 27 November 1837 son of Robert Dunn and Isabel Shanks, married Annie M. Curry in Kentucky during 1865, settled in Washington by 1879, died in Parker Bottom, Washington, on 21 May 1908. [WSP]

DUNSIRE, ANDREW, born in Buckhaven, Fife, late from Glasgow, married Isabella A Ritchie, second daughter of Alexander Ritchie in Bishopmill, Elgin, Morayshire, in Missoula, Montana, on 27 May 1892.[FFP]

DURHAM, EDWARD M., youngest son of James Durham in Edinburgh, married Emily Perkins, youngest daughter of Albert G. Perkins of Franklin, Tennessee, in Kansas City, Missouri, on 17 September 1874. [S#9738]

DURIE, ROBERT, a carpenter in Kansas City, cnf 1893. [NAS.SC70.1.320]

DURNO, Mrs JANE, born in 1803, wife of James Durno late of Aberdeen, died in Upper Alton, Illinois, on 21 August 1841. [AJ#4900]

DUTHIE, JAMES COWE, from Bonnyrig, Midlothian, a bricklayer in Denver, Colorado, cnf 1887. [NAS.SC70.1.261/79]

DU VALRIE, ..., son of Fritz Du Valrie and his wife from Edinburgh, was born in Calton House, Denver City, Colorado, on 24 March 1874. [S#9583]

DYKES, WILLIAM, born 1859, third son of James Dykes, Kirktonhill, Lauder, died in Pueblo, Colorado, on 8 July 1882. [S#12,191]

DYSON, DUNBAR SMITH, born in Kirkcudbright in 1806, settled in New York by 1831, died in New Orleans on 22 December 1848. [ANY#2.27]

EASDALE, ROBERT M., Morrison, Whiteside County, Illinois, married Mary Mackay, second daughter of Donald Mackay in Thurso, Caithness, in Brooklyn on 17 October 1874. [S#9769]

EASTON, AGNES, in San Francisco 12 May 1869. [NAS.RS.Edinburgh.96/266]

EASTON, JOHN, a cabinetmaker in San Francisco, 12 May 1869.[NAS.RS.Edinburgh.96/266]

ECKFORD, ROBERT, from Innerleithen, Peebles-shire, died in Mitchell, Iowa, on 7 March 1872. [S#8948]

EDGAR, WILLIAM J., from Dumfries-shire, married Maggie S. Dickson, youngest daughter of Peter Dickson of Cleveland, Ohio, in Hericon, Dodge County, Wisconsin, on 4 November 1867. [AO]

EDMISTON, MARGARET, possibly from Govan, settled in Albion, Illinois, by 1870. [NAS.SH.2.5.1870]

EDMONSTON, THOMAS, naturalist on the 'California Expedition' of 1846. [NAS.NRAS#0440]

ELLIOT, HENRY ANDERSON, possibly from Edinburgh, settled in Oregon, Washington Territory, by 1868. [NAS.SH.12.10.1868]

ELLIOT, JOHN JEFFREY, possibly from Edinburgh, settled in Oregon, Washington Territory, by 1868. [NAS.SH.12.10.1868]

ELLIOT, JOHN J., son of Ralph Elliot a surgeon in the Royal Navy, died in Cathlamet, Washington, on 8 September 1874. [S#9741]

ELLIOT, RALPH CHARLES, possibly from Edinburgh, settled in Oregon, Washington Territory, by 1868. [NAS.SH.12.10.1868]

ELLIS, JAMES, born in Dunfermline, Fife, on 28 January 1826, married Mary Cram in 1848 and emigrated to USA, settled on Long Island as a gardener for 15 years, later worked as a farmer in Minnesota, died in 1905. [DJ, 28.10.1905]

ENTERKINE, JAMES, born in Girvan, Ayrshire, on 22 August 1850 son of Joseph Enterkine and Janet Logan, married Rachel Miller in Kansas on 17 August 1877, settled in Washington Territory by 1884, died in Chehalis, Washington, on 29 October 1884. [WSP]

EWING, ALEXANDER, died at Cedar Lake, Texas, in September 1869. [S#8172]

EWING, MARGARET, born 10 July 1800, married (1) Moses McClay in Glasgow, emigrated to New York by 1826, settled in Norwegiantown, Pennsylvania, married (2) Andrew Macomber, died in Yakima City, Union Gap, Washington territory, on 15 April 1884. [WSP]

EWING, ROBERT, son of Robert Ewing in Dunbarton, settled as a house builder in San Francisco by 1868. [NAS.SH.12.2.1868]

FAIRGRIEVE, JAMES, born 1861, died in La Crescenta, California, on 10 August 1914. [Prestonkirk g/s]

FAIRGRIEVE, JOHN, born 1784, died in Rockford, Illinois, on 11 March 1874. [S#9577]

FAIRLIE, MARGARET, wife of Robert Fairlie from Greenock, Renfrewshire, died in Naperville, Du Page County, Illinois, on 11 September 1844. [SG#1342]

FARRELL, Dr JOHN, late in New Orleans, died at 48 Great King Street, Edinburgh, 9 February 1854. [EEC#22540]

FARRELL, Mr ....., arrived in San Francisco on 22 February 1852 on board the <u>Hindustan</u>, Captain Pook, from Glasgow. [SFL#3/83]

FARRIES, WILLIAM, born in Ecclefechan, Dumfries-shire, an ironmonger from Lockerbie, Dumfries-shire, died in Detroit on 2 November 1859. [AO]

FARQUHAR, ALEXANDER, born in 1834, son of Robert Farquhar and Margaret Proctor, died in Omaha on 7 May 1873. [Lhanbryde g/s, Morayshire]

FARQUHARSON, ROBERT ALEXANDER, born in 1845, son of Donald Farquharson a postman in Ballater, Aberdeenshire, died in Fort San Juan, Washington Territory, on 29 December 1875.[Glencairn g/s]

FARRELL, Dr JOHN, late of New Orleans, died at 48 Great King Street, Edinburgh, on 9 February 1854. [EEC#22540]

FELL, Mr and Mrs, arrived in San Francisco on 13 July 1851 on board the William, Captain Gellatly, from Glasgow. [SFL#1/175]

FELL, MARGARET RATTRAY, born in 1841, daughter of James Fell [1811-1889] and Margaret Gow [1813-1885], died in Kansas City on 27 October 1880. [Kinloch g/s]

FENWICK, MARJORY, born 1859, daughter of James Fenwick a blacksmith from Leith, died at Turner Junction, Du Page County, Illinois, on 19 January 1874. [S#9535]

FENWICK, WILLIAM, born 1840, of the Iron Foundry in Omaha, died at the house of his father James Fenwick, Turner Junction, Dupage County, Illinois, in 1879, late of Hawthorn, Leith. [S#11,273]

FERGRIEVE, Mrs GEORGE, born 1794, died in Cooksville, Rock County, Wisconsin, on 3 March 1877. [S#10,510]

FERGUS, or LIVINGSTONE, MARGARET, in Edinburg, Iowa, 1861. [NAS.SC48.49.25.61/232]

FERGUSON, ALEXANDER, youngest son of James Ferguson in Thornhill, Muthill, Perthshire, a merchant in New Braufels, Texas, died there on 4 March 1860. [S#1497]

FERGUSON, DAVID, a manufacturer in Kirkcaldy, Fife, then in Waupon, Dodge County, USA, 1853. [NAS.RS.Kirkcaldy.10.66]

FERGUSON, DAVID, son of Drysdale Ferguson and Christian
Forgan in Kirkcaldy, Fife, settled in Waupan, Wisconsin, by
1853.[NAS.SH.5.9.1853]

FERGUSON, DUNCAN, in Idaho, cnf 1894 Edinburgh.
[NAS.SC70.1.1329]

FERGUSON, GEORGE, born in Ayrshire during 1818, died in
Gold Run, California, on 17 July 1851. [W#1260]

FERGUSON, HENRY, youngest son of Archibald Ferguson, 22 St
James Square, Edinburgh, died in New Orleans on 22
October 1859. [CM#21904]

FERGUSON, JAMES, born 1789, emigrated to USA in 1807, a
grazier in Attakapas, Louisiana. [1812]

FERGUSON, JAMES, from Texas, married Marie, daughter of
Gottfried H. Heslet, in Stuttgart, Germany, on 28 October
1848. [EEC#21735]

FERGUSON, JAMES CAMPBELL, a moulder in Chicago by
1896, son of Douglas Ferguson, a moulder in Bonnybridge,
Stirlingshire, who died 18 February 1896.
[NAS.SH.31.3.1896]

FERGUSON, JOHN PROCTOR, in Chicago, cnf Edinburgh 1900.
[NAS.SC70.1.393/119]

FERGUSON, MARGARET MITCHELL, born 1847, wife of
Thomas Fell, late of Coupar Angus, Perthshire, died in
Kansas City, Kansas, on 7 November 1882. [S#12,285]

FERGUSON, ROBERT OLIPHANT, born in 1824, from
Thornhill, Muthill, Perthshire, settled in New Braunfels,
Texas, died there 22 August 1850; his infant daughter
Euphemia, died there on 6 September 1850.
[DGH:31.10.1850][EEC#22034]

FERGUSON, ROBERT, late a merchant in Wigton, Manchester,
Jamaica, second son of Thomas Ferguson, Young Street,
Peebles, formerly of Leith, died in Howard House, Detroit,
Michigan, on 12 September 1855. [NAS.CC8.8.inv.1857]
[EEC#322800]

FERGUSON, THOMAS, second son of James Ferguson of Baledmond, married Charlotte Holderman, in Felix, Illinois, on 23 April 1879. [S#11,182]

FERGUSON,......, daughter of Thomas Ferguson, was born in Felix, Grundy County, Illinois, on 6 May 1880. [S#11,503]

FERRIER, JOHN PLAIN, son of David Ferrier in Edinburgh, settled in Big Oakflat, California, before 1865. [NAS.SH.20.7.1865]

FINDLATOR, JAMES, born in 1853, son of James Findlator in Glenbervie, Kincardineshire, died in Detroit, Michigan, on 23 May 1877. [AJ:25.6.1877]

FINDLAY, DAVID, born on 28 November 1860, son of Captain Andrew Findlay and Jessie Baxter, died in Junction City, Kansas, on 16 November 1886. [Craig Inchbrioch g/s, Montrose]

FINDLAY, THOMAS, born 1813, son of James Findlay (1780-1852) and Barbara Mitchell (1794-1868), died in New Orleans in 1840. [St Clement's g/s, Aberdeen]

FINLAY, ELIZABETH, eldest daughter of William Finlay from Dunfermline, Fife, married James Bayless, a blacksmith, in St Louis on 20 December 1859. [DP]

FINLAY, GAVIN, possibly from Lanarkshire, settled in Utah by 1871. [NAS,SH.3.11.1871]

FINDLAY, JOHN, son of John Findlay and Margaret Fraser in the Isle of Whithorn, Wigtownshire, settled as a joiner in Chicago by 1880. [NAS.SH.6.6.1880]

FINLAY, W. L., born 1838, from 10 St Patrick Square, Edinburgh, chief collector of the New Orleans and Carrolton Railway of New Orleans, died in the wreck of the <u>Anglo Saxon</u> on 27 April 1863. [S#2485]

FINLAY, Mr ..., arrived in San Francisco on 12 April 1851 aboard the <u>Queen of Sheba</u>, Captain Cadell, from Leith. [SFL#1/125]

FINLAY, ..., son of Stewart D. Finlay a joiner late of 4 Bonnington Road, Leith, was born in Shiloh, Cedar County, Iowa, on 9 November 1882. [S#12,288]

FINLAYSON, JAMES, son of James Finlayson a farmer in Friockheim, Angus, a millwright in Payson, Utah, by 1871. [NAS, SH.7.6.1871]

FINLAYSON, WILLIAM THOMAS, second son of Daniel Finlayson, 21 George Street, Edinburgh, died in Detroit in 1879. [EC#29531][S#11,184]; cnf 1879 Edinburgh. [NAS.SC70.1.197/144]

FINNIE, JAMES, son of Thomas Finnie, feuar in Greenock [died in 1838] and Janet Wilson [died 1882], died in San Andreas, California, during 1863. [Gourock, Chapel Street g/s]

FINNIE, JANE, daughter of William Finnie in Linlithgow, West Lothian, wife of Duncan Drummond, settled in Chicago before 1881. [NAS.SH.13.6.1881]

FINNIE, JOHN, a power loom dresser from Glasgow, with his wife Christina Fleming, and daughter Christina, settled in Michigan before 1859. [NAS.SH.20.4.1859]

FINNIS, PETER MURRAY, a clerk in Chicago by 1892, son of Peter Murray Finnis in Edinburgh who died on 16 February 1880. [NAS.SH.5.5.1892]

FISHER, JAMES, born 1837, eldest son of .... Fisher in St Colme's, Dunkeld, Perthshire, died in St Louis, Missouri, on 13 May 1872. [S#9002]

FISHER, JOHN, born in 1805, from Newburgh, Fife, lately a master mariner in Liverpool, died in Ann Arbor, Michigan, on 20 February 1851. [FJ#952]

FISHER, ..., possibly from Edinburgh, settled in Chicago by 1890. [NAS.SH.11.10.1890]

FLECK, THOMAS, probably from Glasgow, settled in Benicia, California, before 1865. [NAS.SH.15.3.1865]

FLEMING, JOHN, eldest son of Robert Fleming, 4 Bank Street, Edinburgh, died in Chicago, Illinois, on 9 February 1882. [S#12,056]

FLETCHER, GEORGE, in Wahoo, Nebraska, 1879. [NAS.NRAS#1345]

FLETCHER, MILES ANGUS, married Martha Cunningham, daughter of David Maitland Makgill Crighton of Rankeillor, Fife, in St Paul, Minnesota, on 16 September 1871. [S#8799]; Miles Angus Fletcher, born 1847, son of George Fletcher late of the Bengal Civil Service, died at Holy Cross, Clay County, Minnesota, on 5 December 1871. [S#8870]

FLETCHER, Reverend WILLIAM, in Iowa and Eldred, Nebraska, 1848-1873. [NAS. NRAS#1345]

FLORENCE, JESSIE A., daughter of Charles R Howden in Dunedin, New Zealand, died in San Francisco on 28 October 1875. [S#10097]

FLOWERDEW, JAMES GRAY, of Hewitt, Flowerdew and Company merchants in Portland, Oregon, died there on 22 July 1872. [S#9065]

FOGO, WILLIAM H. LAURIE, son of Reverend J. Laurie in Rhu, died in Sparland, Marshall Co., Illinois, on 27 September 1876. [S#10,357]

FORBES, ALEXANDER, son of Duncan Forbes [1783-1839] a blacksmith and Isabella Johnston [1792-1874], a merchant in San Francisco. [Old High Church g/s, Inverness]

FORBES, ALEXANDER, a merchant in San Francisco, cnf 1884 Edinburgh. [NAS.SC70.1.230/603]

FORBES, DAVID CRIGHTON, born in Dundee on 12 July 1831 son of John Forbes and Elizabeth Cochrane, married Almira Elizabeth Kennedy in Sammammish County, Washington Territory, on 17 September 1857, settled in Mason County and then in Olympia, Washington Territory, died there on 23 June 1880. [WSP]

FORBES, FRANCIS, born during 1817, son of Sir Charles Forbes, died in San Francisco on 30 December 1849. [AJ#5335][W#1099][GM.NS.33.559]

FORBES, GEORGE COWIE, MD, son of Reverend Lewis Forbes minister of Boharm, Banffshire, died in San Francisco on 3 January 1850.[AJ:12.3.1851]

FORBES, JAMES ALEXANDER, British Vice Consul in Monterey by 1844. [SHR#153/142]

FORBES, JOHN STUART, born 1850, son of Sir William Forbes of Pitsligo, arrived in San Francisco in August 1871, joined the 7th Cavalry in 1872, died at the Battle of the Little Big Horn in June 1876. [S]

FORBES, ROBERT, born in 1855, son of William Forbes and Margaret Hopkins, died in Leadville, Colorado, on 10 December 1891.[St Andrews g/s, Fife]

FORD, THOMAS, born in 1831, son of John Ford in Masterton, Fife, died in San Francisco on 17 April 1863. [DP]

FORKER, ROBERT, an engineer from Dysart, Fife, in Chicago 1892. [NAS.RS.Dysart.7.235]

FORREST, CHARLES STEWART, youngest son of William Forrest an engraver in Edinburgh, died in Austin, Texas, in 1881. [S#11,,945]

FORREST, JAMES, born in 1840, late of Aberdeen and son of George Forrest, formerly a blacksmith at Auchneive, Tarves, Aberdeenshire, died in Chicago on 2 January 1868. [AJ:22.1.1868]

FORREST, PHENICA, daughter of John Forrest, Great Western Mills, Illinois, married John Clay jr., Bow Park, Toronto, in Highland Park, Chicago, on 5 January 1881. [S#11,694]

FORREST, WILLIAM, born in 1847, son of Robert Forrest in Aberdeen, died in Fort Calhoun, Nebraska, on 19 March 1868. [AJ:15.4.1868]

FORRET, ANDREW, son of Thomas Forret in Blebo Craig, Fife, settled as a mason in Chicago before 1877. [NAS.SH.16.11.1877]

FORSTER, MARK, late farmer at Sauchenside Ford near Edinburgh, died in Kankakee City, Illinois, on 23 July 1871. [S#8766]

FORSYTH, CATHERINE, eldest daughter of William Forsyth in Townhill, Dunfermline, Fife, married William Hutton, born in 1857, eldest son of William Hutton an engine driver in Dunfermline, in Ogden, Utah, on 2 June 1891, died in San Francisco on 7 August 1902. [DJ]

FORSYTHE, JOHN, a land agent in Chicago, cnf 1886 Edinburgh. [NAS.SC70.1.253/701]

FOWLER, DONALD, a blacksmith from Nairn, then in Sherman, Texas, by 1882. [NAS.RS.Nairn.6.17]

FOYER, ARCHIBALD EDMONSTON, born in 1861, son of David Foyer and Christina Muir, died in Sumner, Nebraska, during February 1907. [Campsie g/s, Stirlingshire]

FOYER, DAVID MUIR, born in 1862, son of Archibald Foyer a grazier in Knowhead, died in Sutherland, Nebraska, on 8 December 1914.[Campsie g/s, Stirlingshire]

FOYER, WILLIAM, born in 1869, son of David Foyer and Christina Muir, died in Sutherland, Nebraska, on 10 September 1895. [Campsie g/s, Stirlingshire]

FRASER. ANDREW, born in 1882, son of Francis Fraser and Janet Munro, died in Antelope, Oregon, on 21 April 1909. [Suddie g/s, Black Isle]

FRASER, BAILEY SIMPSON, born 1808, late of New Orleans, died in Portobello, Edinburgh, on 16 July 1861.[East Preston Street Cemetery, Edinburgh]

FRASER, DANIEL, Deputy Recorder of St Louis, eldest son of Rev. Daniel Fraser in Helmsdale, died in St Louis on 9 May 1881. [S#11,821]

FRASER, GEORGE, a baker in Chicago, from Munichyne, Ross-shire, married Catherine Ross, daughter of David Ross in Invergordon, in Hoboken, New Jersey, on 6 December 1867. [S#7617]

FRASER, HUGH, born 1856, son of Hugh Fraser a farmer in Lenie, Inverness-shire, died in Texas on 24 October 1879. [S#11,352]

FRASER, JAMES, born 1755, late in Detroit, died in Aberdeen on 4 October 1815, [St Nicholas g/s, Aberdeen]; cnf 14 November 1815 Aberdeen. [NAS.CC1.6.W715]

FRASER, JAMES, in Stockton, California, cnf Edinburgh 1900. [NAS.SC70.1.386/199]

FRASER, JANE, fifth daughter of William Fraser in Clunas, Inverness-shire, and widow of A. Stewart, Woodlands, Nairnshire, married Thomas Hogan of Buckhorn, Louisiana, at Milliken's Bend, Louisiana, on 13 September 1877. [S#10,681][EC#29031]

FRASER, JOANNA, daughter of Donald Fraser and Mary Joyner in Invergordon, Ross and Cromarty, wife of Roderick Mackenzie in Wisconsin 1871. [NAS.SH.10.5.1871]

FRASER, JOHN FERGUSON, born in 1839, son of John Fraser [1809-1878] and Jane McGregor [1809-1865], died Kansas City, 9 November 1922. [Greenock g/s]

FRASER, MAGGIE, daughter of John Fraser a typefounder of McDowall Street, Edinburgh, married John Barr Glen a merchant in Wausan, at Steven's Point, Wisconsin, on 26 August 1873. [S#9420]

FRASER or ROSE, MARY, from Nairn, then in Herman, Grant County, Minnesota, 1897. [NAS.RS.Nairn.21.235]

FRASER, MATTHEW MONCRIEFF, from Glasgow, settled in Kansas City, cnf 1885 Edinburgh. [NAS.SC70.1.239]

FRASER, MAY, third daughter of A. Fraser from Midmills, Inverness, but then Brown Street, St Louis, married A. Mitchell of Emersey, in St Louis on 14 August 1872. [S#9089]

FRASER, PETER, born in Dingwall on 17 February 1834, son of John Fraser [1809-1878] and Jane McGregor [1809-1865], died in San Francisco on 11 May 1862. [Greenock g/s]

FRASER, WILLIAM, youngest son of William Fraser, Clunas, Nairnshire, died in Madison, Millikins bend, Louisiana, on 25 November 1878. [S#11,065]

FRASER, ..., daughter of George Fraser a baker from Munlochy, was born at 406 East Division Street, Chicago, 20 March 1869. [S#8014]

FRASER,....., daughter of George Fraser a baker from Munlochy, was born in Chicago on 4 June 1870. [S#8398]

FREEMAN, JAMES A., Genesee, Waukesha County, Wisconsin, 1870. [NAS.SC48.49.25]

FREW, JOHN MCINTYRE, born 1866, twin son of Archibald and Amelia Cowpar Frew, Guelph, Ontario, died in Kellog Township, Beadle County, Dakota, on 31 July 1884. [S#12829]

FREW, ..., daughter of A. Frew, was born in Chicago on 20 February 1871. [S#8617]

FROOD, JANE, born in 1786, wife of James Wilson from Carthart, Lochmaben, Dumfries-shire, died in Dawson, Sangomo County, Illinois, on 21 March 1861. [AO]

FYFFE, WILLIAM ALLAN, infant son of David Fyffe from Lindertis, Angus, died in Woodstock, Minnesota, on 21 December 1882. [S#12,322]

GAIRNS, ROBERT, son of Andrew Gairns and Janet Johnston in Cupar, Fife, an engineer in Chicago by 1857. [NAS.SH.27.1.1857]

GALEN, MARJORY, born 1846, wife of William R. Walker, died in St Louis, USA, on 16 May 1870. [St Nicholas g/s, Aberdeen]

GALL, WILLIAM, in San Francisco, 1886, son of William Gall a tailor in Fraserburgh, Aberdeenshire, who died 22 May 1884.[NAS.SH.13.3.1886]

GALLOWAY, BARBARA, daughter of George Galloway a farmer in Bankhead, Inchdairnie, Fife, wife of John W. Love, died in Portage, Wisconsin, 5 October 1868. [S#7890]

GAMBLE, JAMES, born in 1780, arrived in America around 1802, a farmer in Genevieve, Missouri. [1812]

GARDINER, JAMES, a tinsmith from Dundee, with his wife and family, settled in Salt Lake City and around 1863 in Minneapolis. [Dundee Archives#GDx58]

GARDINER, MARY, from Kilmarnock, Ayrshire, married Lafayette Allen from Boston, Massachusetts, in Sacramento on 7 June 1860. [S#1604]

GARDNER, JOHN, son of James Gardner in Edinburgh, died in Quincy, Illinois, on 9 March 1882. [S#12,079]

GARIOCH, ALEXANDER, from Edinburgh, a stockbroker and merchant in San Francisco, died there 12 January 1869, [S#8051]; cnf 1889 Edinburgh. [NAS.SC70.1.276/576]

GAVIN, JAMES, 311 East Wayne Street, Fort Wayne, Indiana, 1897. [NAS.SC58.42.61.520, 524]

GEDDES, ALEXANDER, second son of Alexander Geddes in Vinton, Iowa, died in San Francisco on 14 July 1870. [S#8447]

GEDDES, Mrs ELIZABETH, born 1810, wife of Alexander Geddes, died in Vinton, Iowa, on 8 March 1873. [S#9264]

GEDDES, ..., son of Alexander Geddes from Blairmore, Aberdeenshire, was born at 865 Indiana Avenue, Chicago, on 6 November 1878. [S#11,018]

GEDDES, ..., daughter of Alexander Geddes, was born in Hyde Park, Chicago, on 3 August 1883. [S#12,500]

GEMMELL, PETER, settled in Natchez by 1830. [Fenwick g/s, Ayrshire]

GERRON, JOHN, born in 1830, son of Edward Gerron and Agnes Henderson, died in Sacramento City on 16 February 1867. [Whithorn g/s, Wigtownshire]

GIBB, CHARLES LYALL, born on 12 September 1857, son of David Gibb and Helen Valentine, died in Seattle on 15 November 1904. [Abernethy g/s, Perthshire]

GIBB, DANIEL, in San Francisco, married Helen Walker Johnstone, born on 14 November 1839, daughter of Reverend Robert John Walker in Auchtermuchty, Fife, at Logie, Stirlingshire, on 14 November 1855.[F#4/357][EEC#788818]

GIBB, or WEDDERSPOON, SARAH, in San Francisco, cnf 1872 Edinburgh. [NAS.SC70.1.160/367]

GIBB, WILLIAM, a merchant in San Francisco, cnf 1872 Edinburgh. [NAS.SC70.1.160/98]

GIBB, WILLIAM, a mason in San Fransisco, 1872. [NAS.SH.18.1.1872]

GIBSON, AGNES, born 1837, daughter of Hugh Gibson [1813-1894] and Janet Hill, died in Denver, Colorado, 1907. [Kilmarnock, Ayrshire, g/s]

GIBSON, HUGH C., from Leith, married Nellie, daughter of John Ingraham, a shipowner in Detroit, there 19 February 1870. [S#8452]

GIBSON, JAMES TAYLOR, of the firm of John Gibson and Company in New Orleans, died there on 12 February 1849. [SG#18/1804]

GIBSON, JAMES, born in Aberdeen during 1829, a manufacturer, died in Kansas City on 10 April 1875. [AJ:5.5.1875]

GIBSON, JANE, daughter of George Gibson, Plumdon Cottage, Annan, Dumfries-shire, married Edward McAdam, Mission Wool Mills, San Francisco, there on 6 September 1869. [AO]

GIBSON, JOHN, son of Hugh Gibson [1813-1894] and Janet Hill, died in Denver, Colorado, 10 February 1890. [Kilmarnock, Ayrshire, g/s]

GIBSON, ROBERT, born 1833, son of Hugh Gibson [1813-1894] and Janet Hill, died in Denver, Colorado, 1894. [Kilmarnock, Ayrshire, g/s]

GIBSON, W. C., of St Louis, married Amelia H. Hammen, youngest daughter of M. Hammen, in Jefferson City on 21 June 1876. [S#10,287]

GIBSON,......, daughter of William C. Gibson, was born in Mitchell's Grove, Milwaukee, Wisconsin, on 6 January 1880. [S#11,426]

GIBSON, ...,,, son of William C. Gibson, was born in Mitchell's Grove, Milwaukee, Wisconsin, on 16 January 1882. [S#12,032]

GILCHRIST, ANDREW, son of William Gilchrist [1755-1837] and Janet Cameron [1760-1815], died in Pacific Grove, California. [Newmilns g/s, Ayrshire]

GILCHRIST, HELEN, in Pacific Grove, California, daughter of William Gilchrist [1755-1837] and Janet Cameron [1760-1815]. [Newmilns g/s, Ayrshire]

GILCHRIST, JAMES, in San Francisco by 1896, son of John Gilchrist, a cabinetmaker in Rothes, Morayshire, who died 8 September 1895. [NAS.SH.7.2.1896]

GILCHRIST, JOHN, born in 1803, from Flowbank, Dumfries-shire, died in Keokuk County, Iowa, on 21 September 1878. [AO]

GILCHRIST, PETER, born in Newton, Kirkpatrick-Fleming, Dumfries-shire, during 1823, died in Keokuk County, Iowa, on 12 November 1878. [AO]

GILCHRIST, PETER, youngest son of Peter Gilchrist, Newton, Kirkpatrick Fleming, Dumfries-shire, died in North English, Iowa, 27 January 1890. [AO: 21.2.1890]

GILCHRIST, WILLIAM, in Tecumseh, Michigan, married Catherine Swan, eldest daughter of William Swan, Queen

Anne Street, Dunfermline, on 3 February 1846.
[EEC#21304]

GILCHRIST, W., arrived in San Francisco on 13 July 1851 on board
the <u>William</u>, Captain Gellatly, from Glasgow. [SFL#1/175]

GILLESPIE, DAVID, sr., born 1806, from Highlaw, Dumfries-
shire, died at 418 West Madison Street, Chicago, on 20
February 1881. [AO:4.3.1881]

GILLESPIE, JAMES, born 1811, son of David Gillespie, late of
Highlaw, Dumfries, died at 494 Madison Street, Chicago, 16
March 1880. [AO:9.4.1880]

GILLESPIE, SUSAN, born in 1845, youngest daughter of David
Gillespie late of Hughlaw, Lockerbie, Dumfries-shire, wife
of R. C. Moffatt, died at 173 Winchester Avenue, Chicago,
on 1 August 1879. [AO]

GILLESPIE, SUSAN, eldest daughter of Thomas Gillespie, 1019
West Taylor Street, Chicago, married Lewis Deucl, in
Chicago on 20 May 1882. [AO:23.6.1882]

GILLESPIE, SUSAN MCKAY, eldest daughter of Thomas
Gillespie from Lockerbie, Dumfries-shire, died at 502 South
Fairfield Avenue. Chicago, on 29 January 1896.
[AO:14.2.1896]

GILLIS, DUNCAN, born in 1844, eldest daughter of John Gillis in
Glendaruel, Argyllshire, died in Detroit on 10 July
1877.[EC#28969]

GILMOUR, JAMES, probably from Glasgow, settled in Ozark,
Missouri, by 1875. [NAS.SH.6.12.1875]

GILMOUR, JAMES, son of Allan Gilmour in Eaglesham,
Renfrewshire, died in Solano County, California, in 1881.
[NAS.NRAS.0608.T-bk67]

GILMOUR of Mound, JAMES, WS, died on a voyage to
California, cnf 1882 Edinburgh. [NAS.SC70.1.214/569]

GILROY, JOHN, [born Cameron], a Hudson Bay Company
employee who was left at Monterey by a HBC ship in 1814,
a sailor, cooper and rancher.[SHR#153/141]

GIRDWOOD, Reverend JOHN, a Baptist pastor, died in Lafayette, Indiana, on 10 June 1867. [S#7460]

GLASGOW, JAMES, born in Scotland during 1823, died in San Francisco on 11 March 1907. [San Francisco Chronicle, 12.3.1907]

GLASS, JAMES DUNCAN, in California, cnf 1899 Edinburgh. [NAS.SC70.1.379]

GLEN, AGNES, third daughter of James Glen, East House, Newton of Balcanquel, Strathmiglo, Fife, married James Black a joiner, in Chicago on 8 May 1888. [FFP]

GLEN, JAMES, from Glasgow, a merchant in San Francisco, died in January 1856.[NAS.SH.22.6.1865]

GLEN, WALTER, from Kirkliston, West Lothian, settled in Salt Lake City before 1861. [NAS.SH.30.7.1861]

GLENDINNING, ISABELLA, daughter of Jane Glendinning in Edinburgh, wife of David Watt in San Francisco, 1862, later in Grass Valley, Nevada, by 1877. [NAS.SH.22.11.1862; 13.12.1877]

GLENDINNING, Hon. JAMES, of Salt Lake City, born at Outerton farm, Annan, Dumfries-shire, on 3 July 1844, educated in Annan and in New York, migrated from Levensworth to Virginia City, Montana, in 1866, a miner in Alder Gulch, then a merchant in Leesburg, Idaho, moved to Salmon City in 1872, then in 1882 to Salt Lake City, minister of the Utah Legislature. [AO:29.1.1892]

GOLDIE, EDWARD, born in 1815, youngest son of Alexander Goldie a cooper in Wamphrae, Dumfries-shire, died in Chicago on 7 March 1875. [AO]

GOLDIE, ROBERT, son of James Goldie and Helen Taylor, died in Sioux City on 31 March 1876. [Campsie g/s, Stirlingshire]

GOLLENS, ANN HOW, second daughter of Colin Gollens from Dundee, married David Henderson from Perth, in St Louis 1872. [S#9073]

GOODFELLOW, JOHN, born in Hawick, Roxburghshire, during 1842 son of Alexander Scott Goodfellow and Isabella Forrest, married Margaret Agassiz in British Columbia during 1876, later settled in Portland, Oregon, and Seattle, Washington, died there in November 1912. [WSP]

GORDON, ALEXANDER, a botanist in New Orleans and Mobile around 1843. [NAS.GD121.79-82]

GORDON, ALEXANDER, from Aberdeenshire, emigrated to Ohio in 1851, settled in Posheshiek County, Iowa, in 1855. [ENES#1.252]

GORDON, DAVID, from Aberdeenshire, emigrated to Ohio in 1851, settled in Posheshiek County, Iowa, in 1856. [ENES#1.252]

GORDON, ISABELLA, daughter of James Gordon of La Crosse, late of Edinburgh, married William Thompson, in Grand Rapid City 17 October 1860. [S#1706]

GORDON, JAMES, from Edinburgh, died in Wisconsin on 8 October 1860. [S#1678]

GORDON, JOHN, son of Andrew Gordon and Margaret Bell in Cupar, Fife, in Providence Mission, Chicago, by 1870. [NAS.SH.4.4.1870]

GORDON, MAGGIE, from Edinburgh, married Hugh Reid, in Chicago on 7 October 1869. [S#8188]

GORDON, ROBERT M., youngest son of James Gordon an artist in Edinburgh, died at St Joseph, Michigan, on 21 October 1872. [S#9146]

GORDON, ROBINA, born in 1849, wife of James O. Fraser, died in San Francisco on 3 January 1899. [San Francisco Daily Morning Call, 4.1.1899]

GORDON, RODERICK, born 1816, died in San Francisco on 21 September 1851. [St Nicholas g/s, Aberdeen]

GORDON, WILLIAM, son of John Gordon, Loch Dougan, Kelton, Kirkcudbrightshire, died in St Louis, Missouri, on 24 March 1823.[DGC:17.6.1823]

GORDON, WILLIAM, born 1810, a joiner, third son of William
    Gordon a vintner in Montrose, died in New Orleans,
    Louisiana, 27 September 1835. [AJ#4587]

GORDON, WILLIAM, born in 1805, from Gatehouse of Fleet,
    Kirkcudbright, settled in Walnut Grove, Knox County,
    Illinois, died on 4 April 1869. [DGH:26.5.1869]

GOWL, MARGARET ELIZABETH, died in New Orleans on 21
    June 1873. [S#9352]

GRAHAM, CHARLES, born in Canonbie, Dumfries-shire, during
    1837, died in Jamesville, Wisconsin, during 1864. [AO]

GRAHAM, HENRY LANCASTER, in Chicago, died in Argyll, cnf
    Edinburgh 1900. [NAS.SC70.1.390/87]

GRAHAM, JAMES WATT, son of R. B. Graham, painter in
    Edinburgh, married Alice Brown, eldest daughter of R. S.
    Brown, photographer, Brougham Street, Edinburgh, in
    Chicago, Illinois, on 21 July 1882. [S#12,190]

GRANT, ALEXANDER, born in 1734, son of Patrick Grant of
    Glenmoriston, Inverness-shire, served in the Royal Navy and
    from 1757 with Montgomery's Highlanders in America,
    married Therese Barthe on 30 September 1774, and settled in
    Charlotte County, New York, in 1776, died at Grosse Point,
    Detroit, on 18 November 1813. [MAA][GM.84.299]

GRANT, ALEXANDER, from Forfar, Angus, died in Carmil, White
    County, Illinois, on 5 November 1875. [DA#4601]

GRANT, ANN FERGUSON, in Santa Barbara, California, cnf 1892
    Edinburgh. [NAS.SC70.1.307]

GRANT, JOHN, born 1864, son of John Grant, a farmer in Daleigh,
    and Annie Grant, died in Imperial, Nebraska, on 14 June
    1911. [Advie g/s, Morayshire]

GRANT, W. C., in Oregon City, 1851, [NAS.NRAS#770/11/5]

GRAY, ADAM WHYTE, in St Louis, Missouri, 1874.
    [NAS.SH.12.1.1874]

GRAY, JAMES, born 9 November 1815 in Edinburgh, fought at the Battle of San Jacinto, a tinsmith in San Antonio, Texas, in 1850, a merchant there in 1860, died in Florsville on 12 September 1884. [TSHA#20/0536]

GRAY, JAMES, possibly from Aberdeen, settled in San Francisco by 1878. [NAS.SH.22.10.1878]

GRAY, MATTHEW, second son of Mitchell Gray late of East Wemyss, Fife, died in Jozliet, Illinois, on 18 February 1884. [PJ]

GRAY, ROBERT, born in Edinburgh 1820, 'long a resident of New Orleans', died in New York on 29 June 1881. [S#11,853]

GRAY, WILLIAM, Secretary and Inspector of Post Offices, formerly of the Post Office in Aberdeen, died in San Francisco on 14 June 1873.[AJ:17.9.1873]

GREEN, ..., son of A. Green, was born in Galveston, Texas, on 3 July 1877. [S#10,613]

GREENFIELD, DANIEL, late in Inverness, son of Thomas Greenfield, 7 Caremont Place, Edinburgh, died in Detroit on 21 March 1880. [S#11,459]

GREENFIELD, RICHARD BAILEY, infant son of J. B. Greenfield, died in Calistoga, California, on 11 January 1874. [EC#27879]

GREENFIELD, WILLIAM, born in Caithness during 1765, died in Detroit, Michigan, on 16 January 1845. [AJ#5071]

GREENHILL, PETER, son of James Greenhill in Cordon, Abernethy, Perthshire, died in St Louis on 25 April 1875. [EC#28276][S#9925]

GREENSHIELDS, JAMES, born in 1877, son of Robert Greenshields [1851-1908], died in Los Angeles, California, on 6 April 1905. [Patna g/s, Ayrshire]

GREIG or MARTIN, Mrs CATHERINE, Farwell Avenue, Milwaukee, Wisconsin, cnf Edinburgh 1899. [NAS.SC70.1.385/829]

GREIG, CHARLES, a merchant, youngest son of James Greig of Eccles, Writer to the Signet, died in St Paul, Minnesota, on 16 September 1867. [S#7552]

GREIG, ELIZA, born 1848, wife of John Honeyman, and eldest daughter of Robert Myles, Dalgairn, Cupar, Fife, died on Scots Farm, Emerson, Mills County, Iowa, on 15 May 1874. [S#9630]

GREIG, JOHN WHITTET, born 11 September 1813, son of Alexander Greig, Writer to the Signet, [1776-1857] and Jane Whittet [1785-1862], died in New Orleans on 17 January 1848. [St Cuthbert's g/s, Edinburgh]

GREIG, LEWIS BORTHWICK, son of James Greig of Eccles, WS, died in San Francisco on 2 March 1872. [S#8946]

GRIERSON, JAMES, a farmer from Ruthwell, Dumfries-shire, father of Grace Grierson who died at Laporte, Indiana, in July 1843 [DGH:14.9.1843]

GRIERSON, JAMES, born in 1791, son of William Grierson in Lochvale, died at Council Bluff, Iowa, on 19 October 1854. [DGC:1.11.1855]

GRIEVE, Mrs ELLEN, born in 1783, widow of John Grieve a blacksmith, from Johnston Hall, Middlebie, Dumfries-shire, who emigrated to USA around 1834, died in Long Grove, Scott County, Iowa, on 26 September 1874. [AO]

GRIEVE, JAMES JAMIESON, son of John Grieve (1813-1893) a merchant and Jessie Smith (1820-1877), died in Ashland, Wisconsin, 20 July 1903. [North Berwick g/s, East Lothian]

GRIEVE, JOHN, born at Johnston Hall, Middlebie, Dumfries-shire, a blacksmith, settled in Davenport, Iowa, around 1850, died at Long Grove, Scott County, Iowa, on 28 May 1865.[AO]

GRIEVE, JOHN, born in 1807, a blacksmith from Annan, Dumfriesshire, settled in Davenport, Iowa, in 1850, died in Long Grove, Iowa, on 10 September 1875. [EC#28423][AO]

GRUER, JOHN, in Meagher, Montana, cnf 1898 Edinburgh. [NAS.SC70.1.366]

GUNN, DANIEL, born in 1841, second officer of the <u>Cumberland</u>, died in San Francisco on 12 November 1870. [Dunnet g/s, Caithness]

GUNN, DONALD, born 1794, a mason from Portobello, Midlothian, died in Rockford, Illinois, on 27 August 1877. [S#10,658]

GUTH, PETER, born in 1807, from Rothiemay, Banffshire, died in Illinois in 1861. [AJ:29.1.1862]

GUTHRIE, ALEXANDER, from San Francisco, married Mary Swanson, daughter of James Swanson, Marshall Meadows, Berwick-on-Tweed, in London on 10 May 1872. [S#8983]

GUTHRIE, ANN, wife of William Brown late of Ardmuddle, Aberdeenshire, died in Brownsville, Illinois, on 1 July 1849. [AJ#5299]

GUTHRIE, JOHN, born 1841, eldest son of Hugh Guthrie in Kirkcudbright, died in San Francisco, California, on 6 January 1881. [S#12,030]

GUTHRIE, ..., daughter of Alexander Guthrie, was born in San Rafael, California, on 18 February 1873. [EC#27584][S#9235]

GUTHRIE, ..., daughter of Alexander Guthrie, was born in San Rafael, California, on 20 June 1874. [EC#28002][S#9654]

HAIG, JAMES DAVID, late of the Advocates Library, Edinburgh, died in St Louis, Missouri, on 4 March 1873. [S#9292]

HALE, CARRIE BARTON, in Santa Barbara, California, cnf 1894 Edinburgh. [NAS.SC70.1.336]

HALE, DANIEL HORATIO, a broker in Los Angeles, cnf 1888 Edinburgh. [NAS.SC70.1.265]

HAMILTON, ALEXANDER, son of James Hamilton and Jessie Beattie, died in Tenino, Washington, on 26 August 1915. [Dalbeattie g/s, Kirkcudbright-shire]

HAMILTON, ANDREW, born 1849, from Port Glasgow, soldier of the 7th US Cavalry in 1876. [S]

HAMILTON, JAMES, a merchant in New Orleans, 29 August 1834. [NAS.SC37.59.8/69]

HAMILTON, JULIA ARABELLA, born 1829, daughter of James Hamilton, wife of Charles H. Madeley from Liverpool, died in Lacon, Marshall County, Illinois, on 20 October 1860.[S#1686]

HAMILTON, WILLIAM, born in 1836, son of William Hamilton, died on 17April 1867, buried in Chicago. [Galston g/s Ayrshire]

HAMILTON, WILLIAM, from Glasgow and St Boswells, died at North Cape, Wisconsin, on 11 August 1878. [S#10,959]

HANNA, JAMES, from Glasgow, married Rosella C. Jones, daughter of George M. Jones from Templeton, Massachusetts, in St Louis on 25 March 1874. [EC#27960]

HANNAH, DAVID, son of Alexander Hannah {1822-1894} and Mary Morrison {1820-1896}, died in Kansas City during 1888.[Whithorn g/s Wigtownshire]

HANNAY, MARY, from Dumfries, wife of Thomas Affleck, died in Independence, Illinois, on 13 April 1839. [DGH:14.6.1839]

HANNAY, ROBERT MUTER, son of John Hannay in Kirkbride, Kirkmichael, Ayrshire, died in San Antonio, Texas, on 7 December 1848.[DGH:12.4.1849]

HARCUS, ALEXANDER, son of Alexander Harcus a builder in Burntisland, Fife, died in Detroit on 22 August 1873. [EC#27749][S#9401]

HARCUS, MAGGIE, daughter of Reverend F. Harcus from Orkney, married I. Howston from Orkney but settled in Maryville, California, in Port Colborne, Canada, 9 August 1870. [S#8455]

HARDIE, CHARLES ADAMS, formerly a farmer in Dunfermline, Fife, died in Wakonda, South Dakota, on 28 July 1901. [DJ]

HARDIE, GEORGE, son of James Hardie in Sheephousewells, Dunfermline, Fife, married Catherine Auchmuty, daughter of

John Auchmuty in Bowhouse, Wemyss, Fife, at Fowler, Fresno County, California, on 8 April 1891. [DJ]

HARDIE, ..., son of Joseph Hardie, was born in Ross, Iowa, on 11 January 1883. [S#12,340]

HARDIE, THOMAS LISTON, born 1842, son of John Hardie a banker and writer in Linlithgow, West Lothian, died in Gilroy, California, on 14 September 1881. [S#11,934]

HARDIE, WILLIAM, son of Alexander Hardie [1839-1889], died in Blackfoot, Idaho, on 28 May 1912. [Rhynie g/s, Aberdeenshire]

HARDY, JAMES ANDERSON, son of James Hay Hardy, Elizafield, Bonnington, died in Chicago on 18 June 1874. [S#9659]

HARDY, WILLIAM F., married Emma Brent, widow of James Beckham, of Jefferson County, Virginia, in St Louis, Missouri, 18 May 1861. [S#1893]

HARDY, ..., son of William F. Hardy, was born in St Louis, Missouri, on 26 December 1861. [S#2070]

HARDY, ..., son of William Forrester Hardy, was born in St Louis, Missouri, on 6 October 1868. [S#7887]

HARDY, WILLIAM, youngest son of William Forrester Hardy, died in St Louis, Missouri, on 26 April 1869. [S#8048]

HARKNESS, Captain JAMES, born 1829, son of Gregor Harkness [1802-1853] and Isabella Laurie [1804-1878], died in Galveston, Texas, 17 August 1872. [Kilmun g/s, Argyll]

HARLEY, MARGARET, eldest daughter of Joseph Harley a cabinetmaker in Buccleuch Street, Edinburgh, married Robert Rae, in San Francisco on 3 November 1869. [S#8235]

HARPER, Mrs JANE CUMMING, wife of John Harper from Maryhill, Greens, Turriff, Aberdeenshire, died in Marseilles, Illinois, on 8 March 1871. [AJ:5.4.1871]

HARRISON, JOHN, born 1848, only son of Henry Harrison, Scalloway, Shetland Islands, died in New Orleans on 19 November 1867. [S#7606]

HARROWER, ..., son of James Harrower an engineer, was born in San Francisco on 5 September 1876. [S#10,374]

HART, JAMES WILLIAM, in San Francisco, cnf 1900 Edinburgh. [NAS.SC70.1.386/556]

HARVEY, JOHN, son of Charles Harvey in Huntly, Aberdeenshire, a railwayman in Michigan, 1870. [NAS.SH.30.12.1870]

HASTIE, HELEN, possibly from Airdrie, Lanarkshire, wife of … Barnes, settled in Franklin, Indiana, before 1873. [NAS.SH.13.11.1873]

HAWTHORNE, JOSEPH, born in 1862, son of William Hawthorne and Agnes McCulloch, {1823-1906}, died in Ladysmith, Vancouver, on 3 October 1907, and was buried at Great Falls Cemetery, Montana. [Whithorn g/s, Wigtownshire]

HAY, ELIZA, born in 1829, daughter of Reverend William Scott Hay of the Free Church in Midmar, Aberdeenshire, died in Buffalo Grove, USA on 15 April 1859. [AJ:25.5.1859]

HAYES, ALEXANDER, born in Greenock, Renfrewshire, during 1842, died in San Francisco on 18 November 1885. [Daily Alta California, 20.11.1885]

HEATLY, EDWARD, in San Francisco, cnf 1899 Edinburgh. [NAS.SC70.1.384/30]

HEDDERWICK, JANE, wife of John Seth, died in St Louis on 7 July 1873. [S#9362]

HENDERSON, DAVID, from Perth, married Ann How Gollens, second daughter of Colin Gollens from Dundee, in St Louis in 1872. [S#9073]

HENDERSON, JANET, eldest daughter of Joseph Henderson, Clarencefield, married Joseph B. Salmond from Texas, in New Orleans on 31 October 1893. [AO:1.12.1893]

HENDERSON, JOHN, in Louisiana, cnf 1876 Edinburgh.
[NAS.SC70.1.179/857]

HENDERSON, Mrs MARY, from Aberdeen, died at Johnson's
Ranch, Feather, Bute County, in 1851. [AJ:10.12.1851]

HENDERSON, ROBERT, a carpenter and builder, from Lindores,
Fife, emigrated to Canada in April 1883, married Mary
Emma Masterson, eldest daughter of John Masterton a
seaman, in Omaha, Nebraska, on 20 June 1886. [PJ]

HENDERSON, STEPHEN, settled in New Orleans before 1831.
[Dunblane, Perthshire, g/s]

HENDERSON, WALTER, born in March 1844, son of John
Henderson, died in San Francisco in May 1884.
[St Cuthbert's g/s, Edinburgh]

HENDERSON, WILLIAM, in Chicago, son of George Henderson
in Fife-Keith who died 7 December 1888.
[NAS.SH.16.1.1891]

HENDERSON, WILLIAM P., in Coronado, San Diego, 1904.
[NAS.RS.Tain.22.52]

HENDERSON, WILLIAM P., in Coronado, San Diego, California,
1904. [NAS.242/70/22/52.Tain]

HENDRIE, DANIEL, born in Dunbartonshire on 17 June 1835,
emigrated to America in 1851, in San Francisco 1856-1858,
died in Philadelphia on 13 December 1892. [AP#206]

HENDRIE, ROBERT, married Helen Christie from Aberdeen, in
San Francisco on 29 September 1856. [AJ5680]

HENNEN, CAROLINE LOUISE, daughter of Alfred Hennen, wife
of William Mure HM Consul, died in New Orleans on 15
December 1851. [FJ#995][W#1293]

HENYSY, SANTIAGO, born in Scotland during 1753, a sawyer in
San Francisco in 1842. [SF Main Pub.Lib., 1842 census]

HEPBURN, J., in Oregon, 1874. [NAS.NRAS.1021/69]

HEPBURN-MITCHELSON, ELIZABETH MOORE, daughter of Archibald Hepburn-Mitchelson, Middleton, Midlothian, married Charles William Curtis, fourth son of Henry Harper Curtis of Longford, in Littleton, Colorado, on 21 March 1881. [S#11,779]

HERON, GEORGE, in Detroit, 1852. [NAS.SH.15.7.1852]

HERON, J., born 1805, a clerk, emigrated via Port Glasgow on the Jamaica, master John Heron, bound for New Orleans to settle there, arrived 19 January 1829. [USNA#M259/7]

HERON, or MCQUAKER, SARAH, in Henry, Dakota, 1886, sister of Jessie Heron in Barrachan, Wigtownshire, who died 19 October 1885. [NAS.SH.12.5.1886]

HEUGH, WILLIAM, born in 1811, son of Walter Heugh [1776-1854] and Janet Bald [1787-1837], died in Nevada City on 21 August 1867. [Airth g/s, Stirlingshire]

HEWAT, ANDREW, younger son of Peter Hewat, Writer to the Signet in Edinburgh, died in Houston, Texas, in September 1867. [S#7555]

HILL, CLARA VIOLET, daughter of William Hill in New Orleans, married Reverend William Reid, at 4 Forres Street, Edinburgh, on 31 October 1854. [EEC#22653]

HILL, GEORGE, third son of Thomas Hill, Stapleton, Annan, Dumfries-shire, died in San Francisco on 4 May 1876. [AO]

HILL, JAMES, born 1826, from Edinburgh, Sergeant of the 7th US Cavalry in 1876. [S]

HILL, WILLIAM, died in New Orleans 12 November 1826. [AJ#4123]

HODGE, HELEN, in Illinois on 16 October 1875. [NAS.RS.Edinburgh.121/86]

HODGE, THOMAS, born in Crail, Fife, 1814, emigrated to Canada in 1832, merchant in Hamilton, Ontario, moved to Chicago in 1866, died there in January 1896. [FFP.29.2.1896]

HODGERT, JAMES, formerly a joiner in Glasgow, then in Plattemouth, Nebraska, in 1874. [NAS.SC20.34.41.421]

HOGG, ALEXANDER L., in Adams County, Nebraska, 30 July 1878. [NAS.RS.Nairn#12/37]

HOGG, CHARLES, a contractor in St Louis by 1896, son of John Hogg, a joiner in Denny, Stirlingshire, who died 1 July 1894. [NAS.SH.12.8.1896]

HOME, FREDERICK JAMES, born 1852, only son of David James Home and Augusta Home from Dundee, died in New Orleans, Louisiana, on 19 September 1878. [S#10,998]

HOME, JAMES, in Milwaukee, nephew of Mary Home or Matthews in Chapelton Cottage, Auchindoir, who died 8 January 1885. [NAS.SH.7.5.1885]

HOME, LOUIS O., in Missouri on 17 June 1873. [NAS.RS.Edinburgh#12/188]

HOME, WILLIAM F., second son of Robert Home, Gibralter Villa, St Leonard's Hill, Edinburgh, died in Chicago on 21 October 1884. [S#12899]

HOME, WILLIAM RAMSAY, son of James Home in Linhouse, Midcalder, Missouri on 25 February 1871. [S#8629]

HONEYMAN, ..., son of John Honeyman and his wife Eliza Greig, was born on Scots Farm, Emerson, Mills County, Iowa, on 11 May 1874. [S#9630]

HOOD, or TEMPLE, CHRISTINA, in Santa Rosa, California, by 1890, grand-daughter of James Hood, wright in Drybriggs, Cupar, Fife, who died 6 December 1866. [NAS.SH.10.10.1890]

HOOD, DAVID, from Forfar, then in Woodstock, Pipestone County, Minnesota, 1892. [NAS.RS.Forfar.51.230]

HOOD, HELEN, possibly from Ayrshire, wife of Duncan T Galston a machinist in Detroit, Michigan, 1875. [NAS.SH.22.6.1875]

HOOD, JENNIE, in Los Guilicos Ranch, Santa Rosa, California, by 1890, grand-daughter of James Hood, wright in Drybriggs,

Cupar, Fife, who died 6 December 1866.
[NAS.SH.10.10.1890]

HOOD, JOHN, at North Prairie, Wawkesha County, Wisconsin,
1873. [NAS.SC48.49.25.72/119]

HOOD, or SHAW, MARY, in Wildwood Ranch, Santa Rosa,
California, by 1890, grand-daughter of James Hood, wright
in Drybriggs, Cupar, Fife, who died 6 December 1866.
[NAS.SH.10.10.1890]

HOOD, B., born 1842, son of James Hood [1802-1867] and Margaret
Crawford [1802-1836], died in Detroit, Michigan, 11
September 1874. [Kilmarnock, Ayrshire, g/s]

HOOD, THOMAS SHEPHERD, from Cupar, Fife, married Jane
Anne West, daughter of James E. West in Kingston,
Jamaica, and grand-daughter of Mrs Hugh Kennedy of
Batersea, Manchester, Jamaica, at 339 Bryant Street, San
Francisco on 29 October 1881. [S#11,971]

HOOD, ..., daughter of Thomas S. Hood, was born in San
Francisco on 7 January 1884. [S#12,651]

HOPE, H. W., in California, 1881. [NAS.NRAS.1021]

HORN, JOHN, son of John Horn a merchant in Dunfermline, Fife,
settled in Michigan by 1873. [NAS.SH.17.3.1873]

HORNE, Reverend WILLIAM, late of the United Secession
Church in Carnwath, Lanarkshire, died in Yorktown,
Delaware County, Indiana, on 17 December 1848.
[SG#1793]

HORSBURGH, HARRIET EUPHEMIA, fifth daughter of William
Horsburgh, South Queensferry, West Lothian, married James
Dickson, youngest son of John Dickson, Church Street,
Tranent, East Lothian, in Chicago on 28 July 1883.
[S#12,510]

HOUSTON, or WILSON, EUPHEMIA, in York, Nebraska, 1876.
[NAS.SC49.48.25.76/178, 220]

HOWDEN, JAMES, born 1836, a manufacturing and consulting
chemist, youngest son of Matthew Howden and Ann Beath,

50 Minto Street, Edinburgh, died in San Francisco on 6
February 1874. [Edinburgh, New Calton g/s][S#9557]

HOWDEN, WILLIAM, son of Matthew Howden and Ann Beath, 50
Minto Street, Edinburgh, died in San Francisco 18....
[Edinburgh, New Calton g/s]

HOWSTON, I., from Orkney, then in Maryville, California, married
Maggie Harcus, daughter of Reverend F. Harcus from
Orkney, in Port Colborne, Canada, 9 August 1870. [S#8455]

HUME, DONALD, from Kansas, married Catherine Angus
Learmonth, eldest daughter of Robert Learmonth, at
Housebay House, Stronsay, Orkney, on 15 March 1882.
[S#12,072]

HUME, THOMAS JOHN, born 1836, eldest son of Captain
William Hume, died at Eagle Pass, Texas, on 2 August 1878.
[EC#29303]

HUNTER, ALEXANDER, son of Alexander Hunter a cabinetmaker
in Portobello, Edinburgh, died in St Peter's, Minnesota, on
19 August 1862. [S#2320]

HUNTER, GRACE GRIERSON, born in 1865, daughter of David
Hunter and Janet Hamilton, wife of Robert L. Anderson,
died in Ekalaka, Montana, on 28 January 1897. [Anwoth g/s,
Kirkcudbrightshire]

HUNTER, JAMES, born in 1796, from Racks, Tortherwald,
Dumfries-shire, died in Union Grove, Wisconsin, on 26
November 1872. [AO]

HUNTER, JEANNIE, in California, 1898. [Polmont g/s,
Stirlingshire]

HUNTER, JOHN, son of David Hunter a miner in Wellwood,
Dunfermline, Fife, died at Cedar Mountain, Washington, on
9 December 1896. [DJ]

HUNTER, JOHN ROBERT, in Los Angeles, nephew of Robert
Hunter, manager, Agra Bank, Edinburgh, who died 19
December 1890. [NAS.SH.16.6.1891]

HUNTER, Mrs ...., wife of James Hunter, from Racks, Torthorwald, Dumfries-shire, died in Union Grove, Wisconsin, on 11 February 1867. [AO]

HUNTER, ..., son of Colin Hunter, was born in Cheyenne, Wyoming, on 19 December 1881. [S#12,009]

HUNTER, ..., son of Colin Hunter, was born in Cheyenne, Wyoming, on 16 August 1883. [S#12,529]

HUSBAND, BRUCE, son of James Husband a merchant in Dunfermline, Fife, and grandson of Reverend Dr. Husband in Dunfermline, emigrated to America in 1836, an employee of the North American Fur Company and later State Librarian, died in Jackson, Amador County, California, on 5 August 1860. [DP,15.11.1860]

HUTCHISON, HUGH, possibly from Ayrshire, settled in Morrison, Whiteside, Illinois, by 1848. [NAS.SH.4.1.1868]

HUTCHISON, JANE, possibly from Ayrshire, settled in Morrison, Whiteside, Illinois, by 1848. [NAS.SH.4.1.1868]

HUTCHISON, ROBERT, possibly from Ayrshire, settled in Morrison, Whiteside, Illinois, by 1848. [NAS.SH.4.1.1868]

HUTTON, ANDREW, teacher in Platteville, Wisconsin, son of James Hutton in Badger, Wisconsin, who died 5 July 1889. [NAS.SH.5.5.1890]

HUTTON, JAMES, born in 1806, from Dunfermline, Fife, died in Wisconsin on 5 July 1889. [DJ]

HUTTON, MARY, born in 1816, daughter of David Hutton, wife of Robert Hood, died in California on 25 January 1854. [Cupar g/s, Fife]

HUTTON, WILLIAM, born in Canonbie, Dumfries-shire, during 1780, died in Jamesville, Wisconsin, on 28 August 1864. [AO][DGH:14.10.1864]

HUTTON, WILLIAM, born in 1857, eldest son of William Hutton an engine driver in Dunfermline, Fife, settled in Terrace, Utah, married Catherine Forsyth, eldest daughter of William

Forsyth in Townhill, Dunfermline, in Ogden, Utah, on 2 June 1891, died in San Francisco on 7 August 1902. [DJ]

HUTTON, WILLIAM, in Minnesota, grandson of Helen Drysdale or Young in Dunfermline, Fife, who died 9 April 1852. [NAS.SH.8.6.1892]

HYSLOP, JAMES, born in 1803, from Blackwoodridge Limeworks, Middlebie, Dumfries-shire, died at Lake Michigan on 16 September 1857. [AO][DGH:15.1.1851]

HYSLOP, WALTER, from Galashiels, died in Chicago on 16 February 1884. [S#12,684]

IDINGTON, ALEXANDER, born 1843, second son of Peter Idington in Waterloo township, died in San Francisco on 2 April 1871. [S#8671]

INGLIS, JAMES, eldest son of Andrew Inglis the parochial schoolmaster of Dalgetty, Fife, died in St Louis on 2 July 1860. [S#1614]

INGLIS, JOHN, born in Dunfermline, Fife, during 1815, emigrated to California in 1849, settled in Volcano, then in Calaveras County, and later in San Andreas, died in Stockton, California, on 20 November 1880. [DJ, 12.2.1881]

INGLIS, MARY, born in 1886, daughter of George Inglis (1842-1919), wife of George Cameron, died in Spokane on 5 July 1909. [Avoch g/s, Ross and Cromarty]

INGRAM, WILLIAM ALEXANDER, in Dearborn Street, Chicago, cnf Edinburgh 1900. [NAS.SC70.1.395/895]

INNES, ALEXANDER, born in 1830, from Huntly, Aberdeenshire, died at Fort Wallace, Kansas, on 23 September 1868. [AJ:3.3.1869]

INNES, CHARLES LAUDER, born on 20 November 1842, son of Alexander M. Innes and Charlotte Lauder, died at Lake Oregon on 19 March 1908. [Ayton g/s, Berwickshire]

INNES, DAVID KENNEDY, born in 1843, son of David Innes and Elizabeth Stephens, died in Wyoming on 15 August 1879. [Coldstream g/s, Berwickshire]

INNES, HUGH, NS Courts, Chicago, married Annie Scott, in Port Dover, Ontario, on 19 December 1878. [S#11,073]

INNES, ..., son of Hugh Innes of US Courts, was born at 483 West Washington Street, Chicago, on 26 May 1880. [S#11,513]

INNES, JOHN, eldest son of Hugh Innes in Inverness, drowned at the South Branch of Smith's River, near Crescent City, Del Norte County, California, 26 November 1861. [S#2079]

IRELAND, GEORGE, born in 1839, died in San Francisco on 3 February 1864. [Western Cemetery g/s, Dundee]

IRELAND, JAMES, born in 1827, an accountant in San Francisco, son of William Ireland, shipowner, and Euphemia Roger, died in Highland Park, East Oakland, California, on 16 March 1864.
[Ferry-Port-on-Craig g/s, Fife][S#12,712]

IRVING, SAMUEL, from Annan, Dumfries-shire, married Caroline Ross, fourth daughter of Reverend Hugh Ross in Stirling, Nova Scotia, in San Francisco on 26 November 1863. [AO]

JACK, ANNA, daughter of Alexander Jack a merchant in Stoneywood, Denny, Stirlingshire, married George W. Dickie, in San Francisco on 5 August 1873. [S#9395]

JACK, MAGGIE, daughter of John Jack in Edinburgh, married William Scott from Glasgow then in Chicago, at Taylor's Hotel, Jersey City, on 12 October 1873. [S#9442]

JARDINE, ELIZABETH, born in Dumfries-shire during 1799, wife of William Bryden, died in Northampton, Peoria County, Illinois, on 29 January 1870. [AO]

JEFFERSON, DAVID, son of John Jefferson [1806-1847] and Eliza Ogilvy [1813-1863], a shipmaster who was drowned in San Francisco on 16 September 1893 and buried at Laurel Hill Cemetery there.[Arbroath Abbey g/s, Angus]

JEFFREY, JOHN, from Puddledub, Aberdour, Fife, died in Chicago on 17 March 1871. [FH]

JOHNSON, HENRY, born in Glasgow during 1818, died in San Francisco on 30 July 1875. [SF Daily Morning Call, 2.8.1875]

JOHNSON, HENRY W., born in Scotland during 1847, died in San Francisco on 18 July 1879. [SF Daily Morning Call, 20.7.1879]

JOHNSTONE, CHRISTIAN, eldest daughter of Thomas Johnstone in Greenock, married William Graham, Member of the Royal College of Veterinary Surgeons, at Carsonville, Michigan, on 3 November 1892. [AO: 25.11.1892]

JOHNSTON, DAVID, born in 1797, formerly of Allan & Johnston stonecutters in Aberdeen, emigrated around 1842, settled in Madison, died there on 10 May 1857. [AJ:10.6.1857]

JOHNSTON, DAVID HENRY, in Mehama, Oregon, by 1899, son of George Johnston, a manufacturer in East Wemyss, Fife, and his wife Jane Sibbald who died 15 April 1888. [NAS.SH.4.5.1899]

JOHNSTON, GEORGE CHRISTIE, born 1871, son of James Johnston and Alice Jane Christie, from East Wemyss, Fife, and Dundee, died in Scio, Oregon, on 24 January 1905. [FFP]

JOHNSTONE, GRACE, born 1853, wife of John M. Clark, died in Kinglay, Iowa, on 30 March 1887. [AO:22.4.1887]

JOHNSTON, HENRY HAMILTON, born on 23 September 1858, son of Reverend Michael Johnston and Lilias McKechnie, later manager of The Colorado Cattle Company in USA. [F#2/273]

JOHNSTONE, JAMES HOPE STEWART, younger son of Christopher Johnstone late manager of the Caledonian Railway Company, married Agnes Aitchison, elder daughter of William Aitchison, West Bend, Iowa, in Emmetsburg on 28 July 1883. [S#12,513]

JOHNSTON, or RAILEY, Mrs JESSIE, in New Orleans, cnf
Edinburgh 1899. [NAS.SC70.1.383/262]

JOHNSTON, JOHN, at Fort Vancouver, City of Columbia, USA,
probate June 1856 PCC

JOHNSTON, MATTHEW TROTTER, of Victoria and of San
Francisco, son of Adam Johnston of Millknowe, married
Letitia Elizabeth Leggatt, in Victoria, Vancouver Island, on 5
August 1868. [S#7859]

JOHNSTON, QUINTIN, son of Quintin Johnston of Trolorg a
writer in Ayr, settled in Chicago by 1869.
[NAS.SH.3.11.1869]

JOHNSTON, THOMAS, possibly from Stirlingshire, emigrated to
Peoira, Illinois, around 1849, later settled in California.
[NAS.NRAS#0675/3]

JOHNSTON, THOMAS MUNGO, emigrated to Salt Lake Valley
and later on the Cosumnes River near Sacramento,
California, before 1851.[NAS.GD1.277/77/3]

JOHNSTON, WILLIAM, born in 1851, from Turfhill, New Deer,
Aberdeenshire, died in Dwight Township, Livingstone
County, Illinois, on 7 June 1872.
[AJ:3.7.1872]

JONES, OCTAVIA, born 1854, wife of Thomas C. Porteous, died in
New Orleans on 17 December 1882. [S#12,322]

KAY, DAVID, born in 1848, son of Reverend Cathcart Kay and
Elizabeth McWilliam, died in Loup City, Nebraska, on 9
July 1915. [Old Dailly g/s, Ayrshire]

KAY, JOHN G., from Edinburgh, married Agnes, third daughter of
John Watson a merchant in Lawnmarket, Edinburgh, in
Junction City, Kansas, 12 August 1870. [S#8457]

KEAY, ANDREW, a farmer in Terre Haute, Indiana, son of John
Keay (1782-1859), a farmer at Hilton of Carslogie, and
Margaret Melville. [Moonzie g/s, Fife]

KEITH or SCOTT, CATHERINE, sometime in Perth, later in
Texas, inv. 12 November 1889 Perth.
[NAS.SC49.31.134.328]

KEITH, ROBERT, born in Auchingillie, Caithness, during 1800,
died in Fountain City, Wisconsin, on 23 October 1876.
[EC#28788]

KELLIE, Mrs WILLIAM, born in Newton Stewart, Wigtownshire,
during 1803, died in Madison, Wisconsin, on 8 October
1875. [EC#28423]

KEMP, JOHN, a merchant in New Orleans in 1849.
[NAS.SC48.49.48/208]

KENNEDY, JOHN, born in 1848, son of James Kennedy and
Margaret Spalding, died in Redwood City, California, on 20
April 1890. [Kirriemuir g/s, Angus]

KENNEDY, PETER, born 1849, son of Hugh Kennedy farmer
[1811-1876] and Janet McCosh [1813-1910], died in
Buckingham, Iowa, 28 February 1871. [Colmonell g/s,
Ayrshire]

KENNEDY, PETER, from Edinburgh, died in St Louis, Missouri,
on 16 November 1878. [S#11,038]

KENNEDY, ROLAND FERGUSSONE, in Wild Horse Ranch, Big
Springs, Texas, 1884. [NAS.GD60.198]

KENNEDY, ..., daughter of D. Kennedy the Scottish vocalist, was
born in Detroit on 27 December 1868. [AO]

KERR, EDWARD, son of James Kerr in Eildonhall, St Boswell's,
married Sallie Paterson, second daughter of Reverend Dr
Paterson in San Francisco, there on 22 August 1878.
[S#10,992]

KERR, ETHEL MCALPIN, daughter of James W. Kerr, son of
Andrew Kerr, 3 Findhorn Place, Edinburgh, died in San
Francisco on 16 August 1884. [S#12843]

KERR, JAMES WATT, from Edinburgh, married Lizzie Lansing
Bosworth, eldest daughter of S. T. Bosworth, Grass Valley,
Nevada County, California, there on 28 May 1873. [S#9241]

KERR, JAMES W., born in Edinburgh during 1845, died in San Francisco on 22 September 1930. [SF Chronicle, 23.9.1930]

KERR, JOHN, born in 1793, a farmer from Williamwood, Annan, Dumfries-shire, died at Antioch Lake, Illinois, on 31 October 1862.[AO]

KERR, HUGH, born in 1818, son of John Kerr in Calthwaite, Cumberland, and grandson of Hugh Kerr a mason in Annan, Dumfries-shire, died in Georgetown, Eldorado County, California, on 6 February 1862. [AO]

KERR, RICHARD, from Juniper Green, died in Evansville, Illinois, on 18 February 1874. [S#9679]

KERR, ROBERT, born in 1829, son of Robert Kerr [1803-1883] and Agnes Haldane [1798-1888], a Congregationalist minister in Tonah, Kansas, died in Wakefield, Kansas, on 29 June 1890. [Kilmarnock g/s, Ayrshire]; father of Robert, [NAS.SH.21.5.1892]

KERR, WILLIAM, aged 14 months, son of Thomas Kerr in Sharon, Wisconsin, late of Aberdeen, died on 18 September 1847. [AJ#5207]

KERR, WILLIAM, born 1810, from Brycekirk, Dumfries-shire, died in Millburn, Lake County, Illinois, on 29 February 1884. [AO:28.3.1884]

KERR, ..., son of William B. Kerr a harness-maker, was born in Central City, Linn County, Iowa, on 23 July 1876. [AO]

KERR, ..., daughter of James W. Kerr, was born in Grass Valley, Nevada County, California, on 2 February 1874. [S#9567]

KERR, ..., daughter of Edward Kerr, was born in San Francisco, California, on 26 August 1883. [S#12,538]

KESSON, ROBERT, born in 1834, son of William Kesson in Dunfermline, Fife, died in Perrysburg, Wood County, Ohio, on 26 January 1864.[DP]

KEY, JOHN, in Weston, Saunders County, Nebraska, 1910. [NAS.RS.Forfar.75.240]

KEY, WILLIAM I., born in Crail, Fife, 1818, died at 107 Galenne Street, New Orleans, 5 April 1868. [S#7722]

KIDDIE, GEORGE SMALL, born in Dundee on 19 March 1828, married Ann Graham Patterson Clink in Dundee during 1860, emigrated to British Columbia by 1864, settled in Washington Territory in 1868, died in Port Madison, Washington Territory, on 29 July 1875. [WSP]

KINCAID, MARGARET, daughter of Alexander Kincaid, Bowhouse, Stirlingshire, wife of Andrew Weir, Woodside, died in Portage, Wisconsin, on 2 November 1884. [S#12904]

KING, JOHN ROBERT, son of John King an innkeeper in Arbroath, Angus, settled in Jasper City, Iowa, by 1872. [NAS.SH.9.1.1872]

KINGSLEY, CHARLES YORKE, infant son of Maurice and Marie Kingsley, died in Chattanooga, Tennessee, on 28 May 1876. [EC#28617]

KINLOCH, GEORGE, a trader, carpenter and shipbuilder in Monterey, California, by 1844, husband of Mary Anderson a nurse, parents of George David Kinloch. [SHR#153/144]

KINNEAR, JAMES, in Manpun, Fond du Lac, Wisconsin, 1855. [NAS.SC48.49.25.55/201]

KINZIE, JOHN, born 1763, settled in Chicago, died 1828

KIPPEN, JAMES, possibly from Edinburgh, settled in Salt Lake City by 1880.[NAS.SH.16.6.1880]

KIPPEN, ROBERT, born 1850, son of Robert Kippen, 189 London Road, Glasgow, drowned in the Colorado River, Arizona, 23 May 1870. [S#8427]

KIRKWOOD, J., arrived in San Francisco on 22 February 1852 on board the Hindustan, Captain Pook, from Glasgow. [SFL#3/83]

KIRKWOOD, JOHN, in Chicago, cnf 1872 Edinburgh. [NAS.SC70.1.160/562]

KIRKWOOD, N., arrived in San Francisco on 22 February 1852 on board the Hindustan, Captain Pook, from Glasgow. [SFL#3/83]

KNOLLENBERG, FREDERICK, from Edinburgh, died in Richmond, Indiana, on 14 September 1870. [S#8482]

KNOLLENBERG, ROBERT SHAW, born 1847, from Edinburgh, died in Richmond, Indiana, 20 November 1872. [S#9167]

KNOX, HENRY, second son of Alexander Knox in Jedburgh, Roxburghshire, died in Oakland, California, on 28 October 1876.[S#10,403]

KNOX, JOHN BROWN, born on 11 July 1827 son of William Knox and Elizabeth Johnston, married Margaret Buell in Hamilton, Ontario, in 1857, died on Mount Vernon, Washington, 22 February 1909. [WSP]

LADD, ALEXANDER MORRISON, in Oregon, cnf 1893 Edinburgh. [NAS.SC70.1.323]

LAIDLAW, JAMES, born on 23 January 1847 son of Reverend James Laidlaw and Hannah Goodfellow, later the British Consul in Oregon, died on 19 January 1913. [F#2.329]

LAIDLAW, JOHN, son of George Laidlaw, Arthur Street, Edinburgh, died in Chicago on 19 June 1860. [S#1578]

LAIDLAW, JOHN, born on 28 December 1847 son of Reverend James Laidlaw, minister of Wanlockhead parish, and Hannah Goodfellow, later an engineer in Oregon, [F#2.329]

LAMB, CHARLOTTE TAYLOR, youngest daughter of James Lamb, Ruchlaw Muir, East Lothian, died in Glenilly, California, on 27 August 1884. [S#12850]

LAMB, PETER, eldest son of James Lamb a builder in Aberlady, East Lothian, died in Aurora on 19 April 1877. [S#10,549]

LAMB, ROBERT HENRY, son of William Lamb in Galashiels, Selkirkshire, settled in Annawan, Illinois, before 1881. [NAS.SH.1.2.1881]

LAMONT, FLETCHER, in St Louis, cnf 1875 Edinburgh.
[NAS.SC70.1.17/748]

LAMONT, E. N., literary editor of the 'Chicago Inter-Ocean'
married Alice, eldest daughter of James Balfour, Letham,
Leven, Fife, in New York on 5 June 1875. [S#9958]

LAMONT, ..., daughter of Eneas Lamont, was born in Chicago on
28 March 1876. [S#10,213]

LANE, JOHN, from Iowa, married Joanna Jane, elder daughter of
Reverend John B. Munro in Nigg, Ross-shire, at 37 Street,
67th Avenue, New York, 13 May 1874. [S#9626]

LANE, ..., son of John Lane, was born in Burnside, Iowa, on 27
February 1875. [S#9882]

LANE, WILLIAM, from Glasgow, died in Milwaukee, Wisconsin,
on 16 January 1850. [W#1086]

LAURIE, ROBERT, late in Coltbridge, Edinburgh, then in La Porte,
Indiana, married Agnes Peebles, second daughter of Captain
P. Peebles in Pittenweem, Fife, in New York on 22 August
1861. [S#1950]

LAURISTON, ARCHIBALD, eldest son of Archibald Lauriston in
Stockbridge, Edinburgh, married Sarah Crofton, in San
Francisco on 27 September 1874. [S#9754]

LAURISTON, ..., daughter of Archibald Lauriston jr, from
Edinburgh, was born in San Francisco on 13 Janaury 1876.
[S#10,159]

LAURY, Miss..., arrived in San Francisco on 20 October 1852 on
board the Three Sisters, a barque, Captain Douglas, from
Glasgow. [SFL#4/153]

LAW, JAMES COUTTS, born 1862, third son of William Law in
Forfar, died in Chicago in 1884. [S#12845]

LAW, JOHN, youngest son of David Law, Brunton, Cupar, Fife,
died at 90 Seldon Street, Detroit, Michigan, on 13 April
1879. [S#11,172]

LAWRIE, JAMES, a tailor in Milwaukee in 1863.
[NAS.SH.20.1.1863]

LAWRIE, JOHN MCMILLAN, born in 1827, son of Robert Lawrie
{1779-1863}and Elizabeth McMillan {1787-1836}, was
drowned in the Sacramento River, California, in September
1851. [Whithorn g/s, Wigtownshire]

LAWRIE, ..., son of Charles Lawrie, was born at Lake Geneva,
Wisconsin, on 21 October 1883. [S#12,580]

LAWSON, JAMES CHRISTIE, in Kansas, Missouri, 1888.
[NAS.SH.5.9.1888]

LAWSON, ROBERT, in Sacramento, California, in 1870.
[NAS.SH.5.12.1870]

LAWSON, THOMAS, born in 1850, son of Robert Lawson [1818-
1899] a joiner in Coupar Angus, Perthshire, and Jane
Mackenzie [1822-1888], died in San Antonio, Texas, on 2
May 1883. [Coupar Angus g/s]

LAWSON, WILLIAM, son of George Lawson of Cuparhead,
Lanarkshire, settled in Indiana by 1849.
[NAS.SH.16.4.1849]

LAWSON, WILLIAM, from Achavelgin then in Blissfield,
Lenawce County, Michigan, 25 April 1881.
[NAS.RD.Nairn#13/130]

LEE, MARY, from St Patrick Square, Edinburgh, married Henry
Mackie from Edinburgh, in Portland, Oregon, on 2
September 1883. [S#12,524]

LEES, JOHN, died in San Francisco before 1875.
[NAS.SH.21.1.1875]

LEIGHTON, LOCKHART, born in 1803, formerly a schoolmaster
in Strachan, Banchory, Kincardineshire, died in Copley
Township, Knox County, Illinois, in 1858. [AJ:12.1.1859]

LEITCH, DAVID, son of Andrew Leitch in Annan, Dumfries-shire,
died in Chicago in 1894. [AO:30.8.1894]

LEITH, JOHN, born in Leslie, Aberdeenshire, died in Cedar County, Iowa, during January 1868. [AJ:1.4.1868]

LEITH, WILLIAM, born in Leslie, Aberdeenshire, died in Cedar County, Iowa, during May 1867. [AJ:1.4.1868]

LENNOX, MATTHEW, born 1830, son of James Lennox [1794-1862] a sawyer in Kilmarnock, Ayrshire, and Sarah Brown [1802-1863], settled as a farmer in Sacramento County, California, by 1872, died there 31 July 1896. [NAS.SH.4.12.1872][Kilmarnock g/s]

LENNOX, THOMAS, born 1840, son of James Lennox [1794-1862] and Sarah Brown [1802-1863], died in California 16 December 1900. [Kilmarnock g/s]

LENT, ..., daughter of Francis Lent, was born at 1255 State Street, Chicago, on 15 October 1869. [S#8239]

LESLIE, Reverend A., born 1833, second son of John Leslie, 51 Montgomery Street, Edinburgh, died in Allegan, Michigan, on 27 March 1872. [S#8964]

LESLIE, HELEN A., born 1829, wife of James Carter, formerly of Salena, died in Chicago 23 March 1862. [S#2125]

LESLIE, PETER, born in 1820, died in Inland, Adams County, Nebraska, on 12 July 1872. [Arbroath Abbey g/s, Angus]

LESLIE, ROBERT, a mason from West Fenton, east Lothian, died in Chicago 4 October 1869. [S#8190]

LESLIE, WILLIAM, born in 1849, son of James Leslie and Isabel Shearer, died at Lake Michigan on 7 November 1872. [St Peter's g/s, Stronsay]

LIDDELL, HELEN, from Annan, Dumfries-shire, wife of Deputy Sheriff Joseph Roxburgh, died in Benecia, Salona County, California, on 29 April 1871.[AO]

LILLIE, GEORGE E., from 36 St James Square, Edinburgh, married Hulda Milligan of Davenport, Iowa, there 16 September 1869. [S#8171]

LILLIE, Reverend JAMES, born in 1800, from Montrose, Angus, died in Kansas City on 7 October 1875. [EC#28402]

LILLIE, JOHN, son of John Lillie in Greenlaw, Berwickshire, settled as a limeburner in Fort Wayne, Indiana, by 1870. [NAS.SH.6.5.1870]

LILLIE, JOHN, manager of the California Land Investment Company, died in Ariso, Santa Clara County, California, on 12 May 1879. [S#11,197]

LINDSAY, CATHERINE, daughter of Dr Lindsay in Edinburgh, married James Haswell in St Louis 12 July 1861. [S#1941]

LINDSAY, JOHN, born in 1838, died in Will County, Illinois, on 24 December 1871. [Fenwick g/s, Ayrshire]

LINDSAY, JOHN, born in 1870, son of John Lindsay and Elizabeth Esplin, died in Ionapah, Nevada, on 28 October 1918. [Thankerton g/s, Lanarkshire]

LINN, or MCMILLAN, AGNES, in Detroit, Michigan, by 1892, daughter of Robert Linn and Margaret Duff (died 24 February 1886). [NAS.SH.20.2.1892]

LINN, JOHN DUFF, in Detroit, Michigan, by 1892, daughter of Robert Linn and Margaret Duff (died 24 February 1886). [NAS.SH.20.2.1892]

LITTERICK, JOHN, born 1828, son of James Litterick [1804-1873], died in Iowa on 29 February 1912. [Mochrum g/s]

LITTLE, AGNES, second daughter of David Little late of Christilands, Annan, Dumfries-shire, married John Walker, at 1247 Church Street, San Francisco, on 26 July 1893. [AO: 8.9.1893]

LITTLE, GILBERT, born in 1830, son of Archibald and Florence Little, married HelenWalker, settled in Washington Territory by 1860, died in Hadlock, Washington, on 26 December 1910. [WSP]

LITTLE, JOHN, born in 1791, from Limekiln Edge, Hawick, Roxburghshire, died in Jamesville, Wisconsin, in 1865. [AO]

LIVINGSTONE, JOHN, in Edinburg, Iowa, 1861.
[NAS.SC48.49.25.61/232]

LIZARS, MARGARET HOME, born 1789, second daughter of
David Lizars an engraver in Edinburgh, relict of Robert
Armstrong, died in Madison, Indiana, on 14 May 1863.
[S#2494]

LOCKHART, JOHN INNES CRAWFORD, second son of
Norman Lockhart of Tarbrax, died in California on 1
December 1850. [EEC#22095]

LOCKHART, LAURENCE ARCHIBALD, son of Lieutenant
Colonel L. W. M. Lockhart and Katherine Anne Russell,
settled in Colorado before1873. [NAS.SH.17.7.1873]

LOGIE, JAMES, on Saurie's Island, Columbia, Oregon, died in
April 1854, cnf 1855. [NAS.SC70.1.88]

LOGG, GEORGE, born in Galston, Ayrshire, on 24 June 1851, son
of John Logg and Jean Jamie, married Emili Peterson in
Georgetown, Colorado, in 1882, settled in Washington
Territory by 1889, died on Rolling Bay Island, Washington,
on 15 December 1938. [WSP]

LONIE, CHARLES, a joiner from Edinburgh, married Helen,
youngest daughter of Matthew Smith, Easter Bush,
Edinburgh, in Kansas City on 30 November 1870. [S#8556]

LONIE, JANET, wife of Charles U. Stobie, died in Chicago on 10
January 1870. [S#8275]

LOOKUP, ALEXANDER, born in Dumfries 1786, Convenor of the
Seven Incorporations, Magistrate of Dumfries, elder of St
Michael's Church, died in Columbus, Texas, 24 June 1849.
[SG#1847]

LORIMER, HENRY JAMES, born in 1854, son of George Lorimer
and Margaret Wilkie, died in San Jose, California, on 17
September 1891.
[St Cuthbert's g/s, Edinburgh]; cnf 1895. [NAS.SC70.1.339]

LORIMER, J. S., from Glasgow, but in Detroit, married Annie
King, from Glasgow, in Chatham, Canada West, there on 6
November 1860. [S#1701]

LOVE, JEAN, born in 1856, eldest daughter of James Love a farmer in Iowa late from Kilbarchan, Renfrewshire, died on 26 November 1873.[EC#27833]

LOVE, THOMAS, jr., an ironfounder in Chicago, 1876. [NAS.SH.4.3.1876]

LOW, JAMES, son of James Low [1794-1859] and Elizabeth Young [died in 1831], settled in Salt Lake City by 1881. [Holy Rude g/s, Stirling]

LOWE, ISABELLA ELIZA, youngest daughter of John Lowe an engineer in Detroit, Michigan, married John Borrie in Birnam, Perthshire, at Ballinluig on 12 September 1877. [S#10,656]

LOWE, JAMES, born 1830, died in San Francisco on 2 February 1879. [S#11,110]

LUNDIE, MARY, born in 1841, daughter of Andrew Lundie and Jane Ruxton, died in Denver, Colorado, on 30 July 1885. [Arbroath Abbey g/s, Angus]

LYLE, THOMAS, in Lapeer, Michigan, by 1896, brother of Ann Lyle in Monkton who died 15 November 1888. [NAS.SH.29.8.1896]

LYNCH, JOHN, from Arbroath, Angus, then a sheep farmer in Montana, cnf Edinburgh 1901. [NAS.SC70.1.403/1017]

MACADAM, ALEXANDER, a merchant, son of Peter MacAdam in Watten, Caithness, died in Detroit on 13 April 1872. [S#8676]

MCADAM, ..., son of E. McAdam, was born in Sanscombe Street, San Francisco, on 15 August 1872. [AO]

MACANDREW, COLIN, a medical student, son of ....MacAndrew an architect in Aberdeen, died in Georgetown, Texas, on 28 April 1875. [AJ.26.5.1875]

MCARTHUR, JOHN, in Johnstown Center, Wisconsin, 1872. [NAS.SH.10.6.1872]

MACARTNEY, ALEXA, wife of Mathew Watson from Bridgend, Liberton, Edinburgh, died in Brownsville, Cherokee County, Kansas, on 21 April 1882. [S#12,114]

MCBEAN, ALLAN, son of Allan McBean, a farmer in Boggiewell, and Catherine Mackay, died in Zortman, Montana, on 8 January 1912. [Suddie g/s, Black Isle]

MCCALL, W. R., from Dunfermline and Aberfeldy, died at his uncle D. McGregor's residence in Houston, Texas, on 26 September 1873. [S#9447]

MCCALLUM, ISABELLA, born in 1849, daughter of Duncan McCallum and Amelia Cruickshank, died in Kansas City on 1 March 1899.[Fetteresso g/s, Kincardineshire]

MCCALLUM, JANET, in Fillimore County, Minnesota, 3 February 1875.[EUL: Gen#748]

MCCALLUM, JOHN, in Fillimore County, Minnesota, 3 February 1875.[EUL: Gen#748]

MCCALLUM or MCLAREN, M., in St Clair County, Michigan, cnf 1876 Edinburgh. [NAS.SC70.1.180/204]

MCCALLUM, PETER, born in 1837, an architect from Perth and Dunfermline, died in St Louis on 8 May 1887. [FFP]

MCCALLUM, PETER, born in Dunbarton on 12 January 1849, son of Robert McCallum and Ann McKay, married Sarah Harrison in Webster County, Iowa, during 1875, settled in Pomeroy, Iowa, and later in Kittitas County, Washington, died there on 19 March 1911. [WSP]

MCCALLUM, PETER, born in 1860, eldest son of the above, died at Honey Bend, Illinois, in 1882. [FH, 12.10.1882]

MCCALLUM, ROBERT PRESTON, in Fillmore County, Minnesota, died in Preston, Minnesota, 27 June 1873, cnf 8 February 1876 Edinburgh [NAS.SC70.1.176/834]

MCCANN, ..., daughter of William McCann from Edinburgh, was born in Macanville, Woodstock, Pipestone County, Minnesota, on 20 August 1883. [S#12,528]

MCCARTER, JAMES, in Willard City, Utah, cnf 1883 Edinburgh.
[NAS.SC70.1.221/930]

MCCAW, WILLIAM, son of Robert McCaw [1817-1876] and
Jessie McTier [1820-1901], died in Richmond, Illinois, aged
68. [Colmonell g/s, Ayrshire]

MCCLELLAN, JULIA C., wife of D. McGregor, died in Houston,
Texas, on 14 February 1873. [S#9250]

MCCLELLAND, JOHN, born in 1810, son of John McClelland in
Fordbank, a merchant in Charleston, Ilinois, died 10
September 1842. [Wigtown g/s]

MCCLOUD, D., arrived in San Francisco from Glasgow on board
the barque Madeira, Captain Douglas, on 9 November 1851.
[SFL#3/2]

MCCOMB, SARAH, in Detroit, 1819. [NAS.GD176/2027]

MCCOMBIE, RACHEL, wife of John Duthie, died in Los Animos,
Colorado, on 18 December 1891. [Tough g/s,
Aberdeenshire]

MCCONACHIE, ALEXANDER, born in Glenrinnes, Banffshire,
on 7 July 1840, married Sarah C. Mason in Lima, Ohio, in
1870, died in Port Angeles, Clallam, Washington, during
February 1927. [WSP]

MACCORRY, HENRY STUART, ' many years a resident of New
Orleans', died at Bay St Louis, Mississippi, on 17 February
1875. [S#9873]

MCCOUL, WILLIAM CAMPBELL, born in 1824, son of David
McCoul and Margaret Campbell, died in California on 16
February 1850. [Crossmichael g/s, Kirkcudbrightshire]

MCCULLAGH, A., born 1804, a clerk, emigrated via Port Glasgow
on the Elizabeth, master A. Grierson, bound for New Orlean
to settle in Louisiana, arrived in New Orleans 12 November
1827. [USNA.M259/7]

MCCULLOCH, ALFRED LANGDON BRANDER, in Jamesville,
Wisconsin, cnf Edinburgh 1898. [NAS.SC70.1.407/120]

MCCULLOCH, WILLIAM, youngest son of Henry McCulloch of Glenquicken, Kirkcudbrightshire, married Mrs Jennie Luther, in Denver, Colorado, on 14 February 1877. [EC#288861]

MCCULLOCH, WILLIAM, in Kansas Missouri (sic), brother of David McCulloch a merchant in Hong Kong who died 30 June 1891. [NAS.SH.24.11.1892]

MCCULLOCH, WILLIAM, born in 1846, son of Henry McCulloch, died in Kansas on 1 January 1912. [Kirkandrews g/s]

MCDADE, JAMES, born in 1854, son of Robert McDade and Jessie McLachlan, died in Virginia City, Nevada, on 26 May 1896.[Anwoth g/s, Kirkcudbrightshire]

MCDADE, WILLIAM, born in 1859, son of Robert McDade and Jessie McLachlan, died in Virginia City, Nevada, on 7 January 1889.[Anwoth g/s, Kirkcudbrightshire]

MCDONALD, DONALD, son of John McDonald the tacksman of Scalpaig, and Barbara Tolmie, emigrated via Liverpool to New York in 1840, settled in Cedar Keys, Florida, then a book-keeper in Charleston, South Carolina, moved to Corpus Christi, Texas, in 1846, died after September 1878. [NAS.GD403.70]

MCDONALD, J. J., arrived in San Francisco from Glasgow on board the barque Madeira, Captain Douglas, on 9 November 1851. [SFL#3/2]

MCDONALD, MARIAN ISABELLA, from Galashiels, married John S. Roberts Clark of Ranch Healdsburg, in San Francisco on 28 June 1870. [S#8420]

MACDONALD, MARY BROWN, fourth daughter of J. B. MacDonald a planter in Grenada, formerly of Stewart Hall, Bute, married H. C. Hartley of Springfield, Ohio, in Cincinatti, Ohio, on 6 February 1878. [S#10,798]

MACDONALD, NEIL, born 1857, second son of Murdo Macdonald clerk of works to the Lewis Estate, Stornaway, clerk in the London and San Francisco Bank, San Francisco, died at sea bound from New York to Liverpool aboard the Adriatic on 18 October 1883. [S#12,580]

MCDONALD, WILLIAM, son of John McDonald the tacksman of Scalpaig, and Barbara Tolmie, emigrated to Mobile in 1838, settled in St Marks, Florida, in 1840, by 1844 he was in Newport, Florida, later in Georgia, died in Brownsville, Texas, in 1850. [NAS.GD403.70]

MCDONALD, ..., born 1799, a farmer, emigrated via Port Glasgow on the Jamaica, master John Heron, bound for New Orleans to settle there, arrived 19 January 1829. [USNA.M259/7]

MACDONELL, WILLIAM, born in 1851, brother of James MacDonell in London, died in Chicago on 13 May 1879. [EC#29545]

MCDOUGALD, Mrs ISABELLA, born in Scotland 1796, wife of John McDougald, settled in Cumberland County, NC, moved to Texas in 1860, died in Austin County, Texas, 13 February 1868. [NC.Presb:7.10.1868]

MCDOUGALL, DUNCAN, son of Malcolm McDougall [1802-1832], a and Ann Livingston [1804-1873], died in Virginia City, Nevada, on 28 April 1891. [Rothesay g/s, Bute]

MCDOUGALL, F. D., in Maryville, California, 1857. [NAS.NRAS.0853/6]

MCEACHRAN, JESSIE JARDINE, second daughter of Neil McEachran, Gleneden, Bothwell, Lanarkshire, married Hugh R. Robertson of Crookston, Minnesota, eldest son of John Robertson from Bothwell Park, Bothwell, in New York on 29 August 1883. [S#12,523]

MCEWAN, DUNCAN, born 1818, son of Hugh McEwan (1785-1834) a mason in Dunkeld and Christian McCullam (1783-1861), died in Detroit on 27 July 1856. [Little Dunkeld g/s, Perthshire]

MCFARLANE, or BENNET, ANN ELIZA, in Grangeville, California, 1887. [NAS.SH.17.2.1887]

MCFARLANE, JAMES, in Mitchellville Park, Iowa, 1871. [NAS.SH.11.7.1871]

MCFARLANE, JOHN, from Dumfries-shire, died in Brockway, St Clair, Michigan, in October 1886. [AO:17.12.1886]

MCGARTH, MARY ANNE, daughter of Tweedie McGarth, The Bield, Peebles-shire, married Thomas Amos, Etna, Siskiyou, California, at Russ House, San Francisco, on 31 July 1876. [S#10,327]

MCGINNES, JAMES, born in 1839, died in Morgan County, Illinois, on 8 October 1867. [Auchenleck g/s, Ayrshire]

MCGLASHAN, JOHN, son of William McGlashan in Edinburgh, settled in Feliz Valley, California, by 1863. [NAS.SH.12.1.1863]

MCGOUN, DUNCAN, possibly from Renfrewshire, died at Rio Seco, Texas, during 1850. [NAS.SH.23.1.1871]

MCGOWN, or MCMILLAN, ANN CRAIG, in Manistee, Michigan, daughter of John McGown a weaver in Airdrie, Lanarkshire, who died 17 February 1885. [NAS.SH.11.5.1892]

MCGOWAN, MARGARET JANE, possibly from Wigtownshire, wife of ....Sproull, settled in Washington, Iowa, by 1881. [NAS.SH.6.10.1881]

MCGREGOR, DANIEL, born in Lismore, Argyll, around 1832, son of John McGregor, emigrated to Texas 1855, died in Austin, Arkansas, 13 September 1862. [NC Presbyterian: 22.11.1862]

MCGREGOR, JAMES, a farmer from Torenbuie, Strathdon, Aberdeenshire, died at his home on the Ontonogan River, Lake Superior, Michigan, on 27 May 1859. [AJ:14.8.1859]

MCGREGOR, JAMES, a merchant in New Orleans in 1864. [NAS.SC48.49.25.65/191]

MCGREGOR, JOHN, born 1 December 1797, son of Thomas Mc Gregor and Margaret McLaren in the parish of Dull, Perthshire, emigrated via Oban, Argyll, to Charlottetown, Prince Edward Island, on 6 October 1808, a piper, settled in Nacagdoches, Texas, sergeant and cannoneer, fought at the

Battle of Bexar in December 1835, died at the Alamo, Texas, on 6 March 1836. [Sgen.39.2.84][DRTL][Dull OPR]

MCGREGOR, JOHN, in Visalia, California, cnf 1876 Edinburgh. [NAS.SC70.1.179]

MCINROY, CHARLES HESKETH, born on 6 November 1860, son of William McInroy of Lude, died in Spokane on 8 November 1910.[Kilmaveonaig g/s, Blair Atholl, Perthshire]

MCINROY, HENRY, born in 1841, son of James Patrick McInroy of Lude and Margaret Seaton Lillie, died in Colorado on 12 June 1902. [Kilmaveonaig g/s, Blair Atholl, Perthshire]

MCINROY, PATRICK, born on 16 July 1845, son of James Patrick McInroy of Lude and Margaret Seaton Lillie, died in Pueblo, Colorado, on 12 November 1882. [Kilmaveonaig g/s, Blair Atholl, Perthshire] [S#12,291]

MCINROY, PATRICK, youngest son of James Patrick McInroy of Lude, Perthshire, married Amelia Annie, second daughter of H. H. Curtis, at Oaklands Hall, Douglas County, Colorado, on 23 November 1872. [S#9177]

MCINROY, ..., daughter of Patrick McInroy was born at The Spring, Colorado, on 26 August 1873. [EC#27764]

MCINROY, ..., son of Patrick McInroy, was born at the Springs, Castlerock, Colorado, on 18 December 1875. [EC#28484][S#10,136]

MCINTOSH, ALEXANDER, Munroe County, Michigan, 1835. [NAS.GD176/2064]

MCINTOSH, ANGUS, at River Rouge, Michigan, 1820. [NAS.GD176.2015]

MCINTOSH, CATHERINE, in Detroit, 1837. [NAS.GD176/2222]

MCINTOSH, DONALD, born 1834, son of Alexander McIntosh in Nairn, died in Duluth, Lake Superior, in 1870. [S#8472]

MACINTOSH, GEORGE DONALD, fourth son of James Macintosh of Lamancha, married Grace, only daughter of

Robert Kirk, and widow of William Gordon, in Altona, Knox County, Illinois, on 5 September 1871. [S#8809]

MCINTOSH, MARY MCGREGOR, only daughter of Duncan McIntosh late of New Orleans, married James McMillan in Glasgow on 16 November 1875. [EC#28437]

MCINTOSH, WILLIAM, in Indiana and Illinois before 1878. [NAS.GD176/2573]

MCINTOSH, WILLIAM, in Tacoma, Washington, cnf 1892. [NAS.SC70.1.311]

MCINTOSH,......., son of W. K. Mcintosh, was born in Vernon, Thawassie County, Michigan, on 18 May 1874. [S#9637]

MCINTYRE, ARCHIBALD CAMPBELL, born 1843, from Clunes, Lochaber, died in Michigan 1872. [S#9124]

MCINTYRE, PETER, born in Stirlingshire during 1813, a resident of Columbus, Wisconsin, died in Chicago on 10 January 1873. [EC#27565]

MACK, ANNE LOGAN, third daughter of James Mack in Upper Keith, married Thomas, second son of Thomas Carrick in Wooleyburnfoot, Northumberland, in Victoria, Kansas, on 23 January 1879. [S#11,102]

MACK, JOHN, son of Hamilton Mack a farmer in Westinghouse, Carluke, Lanarkshire, settled as a farmer in Pyson, Illinois, by 1880.[NAS.SH.5.1.1880]

MACKAY, ELIZABETH, eldest daughter of Findlay Mackay in Caithness, married Andrew Taylor from Caithness, in Rampart Street, New Orleans, on 11 March 1874. [S#9581]

MACKAY, GEORGE SINCLAIR, born in 1868, son of James Mackay and Jessie Sutherland, died in Oklahoma City on 2 September 1889.[Halkirk g/s, Caithness]

MCKAY, GEORGE R., in Decatur, Michigan, 1896. [NAS.242/70/17/283.Tain]

MACKAY, JAMES, born in Kildonan, Sutherland, 1759, son of George Mackay and his wife Elizabeth McDonald, emigrated to Canada in 1776, an explorer for the Spanish in Louisiana, after 1800 an explorer, militia officer and politician in Missouri, died 16 March 1822.

MACKAY, MARY, second daughter of Donald Mackay in Thurso, Caithness, married Robert M. Easdale, Morrion, Whiteside County, Illinois, in Brooklyn on 17 October 1874. [EC#28117]

MACKAY, ROBERT, a watchman of the Pacific Railroad Company, Valligo, California, cnf 1881 Edinburgh. [NAS.SC70.1.211/595]

MCKAY, SAMUEL, died in White Pine, Nevada, 1872. [S#8917]

MACKAY, SHERIDAN K, a barrister, second son of T. M. Mackay, died in Northfield, Minnesota, 6 August 1867. [GM.ns2/15/97]

MCKEAN, ALEXANDER CHARLES, third son of William Blair McKean [1799-1875], Writer to the Signet in Edinburgh, and Marianne McCulloch, died in San Francisco during August 1869 [Greyfriars g/s, Edinburgh][S#8161]

MCKEAN, ..., daughter of Alexander C. McKean, was born in San Francisco on 15 February 1863. [S#2432]

MCKEAN, ELIZABETH, in Salt Lake City, cnf 1888 Edinburgh. [NAS.SC70.1.265]

MACKENZIE, ALEXANDER CALDER, son of Allan Mackenzie, Braes of Castle Grant, Morayshire, married Annie Mackenzie, youngest daughter of Lachlan Mackenzie, Braes of Castle Grant, in St Paul, Minnesota, on 28 October 1874. [S#9773]

MCKENZIE, HUGH, born in 1845, son of Alexander McKenzie and Christine Grant, chief officer of the US barque Soloman, died in San Francisco on 10 December 1873. [Golspie g/s, Sutherland]

MACKENZIE, J. M., in Detroit 1887. [NAS.GD176/2675]

MACKENZIE, JAMES MITCHELL, second son of Robert Hall
MacKenzie in Cincinatti, died in Vincennes, Indiana, on 13
February 1879. [EC#29465][S#11117]

MCKENZIE, JAMES, settled in Kansas City and by 1889 was
general manager of the Cresswell Ranch. [TSHA#22/0482]

MCKENZIE, JOHN, a baker in Columbia, USA, in 1850.
[NAS.SH.4.11.1850]

MACKENZIE, JOHN, born 1830, son of Roderick Mackenzie
[1796-1844] and Euphemia Mackenzie [1795-1887], died in
Chicago 29 July 1864. [Edinburgh, New Calton g/s]

MCKENZIE, JOHN, a stonecutter who settled in Minneapolis,
Minnesota, by 30 March 1884. [NAS.RS.Nairn#15/232]

MCKENZIE, JOHN, son of Donald McKenzie [1758-1846], a
farmer in Balnagra, and Ann McKenzie [1773-1854], settled
in California.[Lochcarron g/s, Wester Ross]

MCKENZIE, JOHN, from Ross-shire, settled in San Francisco, cnf
1886 Edinburgh. [NAS.SC70.1.253/833]

MACKENZIE, KENNETH, born in Ross & Cromarty 15 April
1797 son of Alexander and Isabella Mackenzie, emigrated to
Canada in 1816, a fur trader and merchant in Missouri after
1822, married Mary Marshall 20 June 1842, died 26 April
1861.

MCKENZIE, MURDO, a bank agent from Tain, Ross-shire, settled
in Colorado by 1882, manager of the Prairie Cattle Company
in Trinidad, Colorado, 1885, manager of the Matador ranch
in 1890. [NAS.242/70/12/123,Tain][TSHA.10.0/555]

MACKENZIE, Mrs R., in Port Oxford, Oregon, 1890.
[NAS.GD176.3026]

MCKENZIE, ROBERT BRYDEN, third son of Reverend James
McKenzie in Dunfermline, Fife, died in Walla Walla,
Washington State, on 31 March 1908. [DJ]

MCKERROW, WILLIAM, in Arcada, Wyoming, by 1889, possibly
from Auchenleck, Ayrshire. [NAS.SH.1.4.1889]

MACKIE, AGNES, born in 1847, daughter of John Mackie and Mary Clark, died in Detroit on 9 July 1875. [Arbroath Abbey g/s, Angus]

MACKIE, HENRY, in Portland, Oregon, brother of David Scott Mackie in Edinburgh who died 7 November 1887. [NAS.SH.11.5.1888]

MACKIE, ISABELLA, born in 1845, daughter of John Mackie and Mary Clark, died in Detroit on 15 February 1879. [Arbroath Abbey g/s, Angus]

MACKIE, JAMES, possibly from Macduff, Banffshire, in Ogemaw, Michigan, by 1890. [NAS.SH.12.8.1890]

MAKIE, JAMES, at Fort William, Franklyn County, Missouri, 1854. [NAS.RS.Forfar.17.228]

MCKIE, WILLIAM, son of William McKie [1776-1849] and Janet McMurray [1785-1831], died in Illinois 14 September 1847. [Barr g/s, Ayrshire]

MCKINLAY, DAVID, born in 1851, son of Alexander McKinlay, Grieve Street, Dunfermline, Fife, died in Dubaque, Iowa, on 14 July 1873. [DJ]

MCKINLEY, JAMES, son of Catherine McKinley in Stirling, arrived in California on a whaler in 1827, settled in San Francisco in 1841 as a mercantile agent. [SHR#153/139]

MACKINNON, ALEXANDER S. B., born 1851, younger son of Reverend Alexander Mackinnon in Strathfillan, died in Milwaukee, Wisconsin, on 13 September 1884. [S#12861]

MACKINTOSH, CHARLES, son of Alexander Mackintosh and Christina MacRae, died in Fort Collins, Colorado, in 1925. [Suddie g/s, Ross and Cromarty]

MACINTOSH, EDWARD 'MANUEL', from Inverness, arrived in Monterey, California, in 1822, settled at Estero Americano Rancho near Bodega Bay. [SHR#153/141]

MACKINTOSH, ROBERT, son of Alexander Mackintosh and Christina MacRae, died in San Jose, California, in 1920. [Suddie g/s, Ross and Cromarty]

MCINTYRE, DONALD, Broadway, Milwaukee, Wisconsin, 1876.
[NAS.SC48.49.25.75/199]

MCKENZIE, ..., son of John McKenzie, was born in San
Francisco, California, on 11 August 1883. [S#12,523]

MCKERRELL, WILLIAM, in Dallas, Texas, cnf 1874 Edinburgh.
[NAS.SC70.1.170/910]

MACKIE, HENRY, from Edinburgh, married Mary Lee, St Patrick
Square, Edinburgh, in Portland, Oregon, on 2 September
1883. [S#12,524]

MCKNIGHT, ALEXANDER, born in 1830, son of Robert
McKnight and Jane McLean, died in Gothenburg, Nebraska,
on 25 January 1897. [Buittle g/s, Kirkcudbrightshire]

MCKNIGHT, JAMES, a busdriver in Coatbridge, Lanarkshire,
formerly in Kansas, cnf Edinburgh 1899.
[NAS.SC70.1.378/313]

MCLACHLAN, HUGH, Goosepoint, married Jane Hope, eldest
daughter of George Hope, Chatham, Oregon, in Detroit,
Michigan, on 8 July 1895. [AO: 2.8.1895]

MCLAGEN, Mrs BARBARA, wife of William McLagen, born in
Broughty Ferry, Dundee, during 1836, died in San Francisco
on 14 February 1884.[San Francisco Chronicle, 17.2.1884]

MACLAGAN, ..., son of Gilbert C. MacLagan, was born in Le
Mars, Iowa, on 24 January 1883. [S#12,363]

MCLAREN, DOUGALD, born in 1849, an ironmoulder from
Dunfermline, Fife, died in Chicago on 26 October 1889. [DJ]

MCLAUGHLIN, Dr JOHN, in Oregon City, 1848.
[NAS.GD121.247]

MCLAWS, JANE, in Salt Lake City, cnf 1895 Edinburgh.
[NAS.SC70.1.342]

MCLEA, DONALD, born in Urrey, Ross-shire, during September
1816, husband of Ann ...., father of Alexander, James,

Arthur, Donald, Annie, Belle, and Mary, died in San
Francisco during November 1885

MCLEAN, AGNES, from Edinburgh, settled in San Francisco, cnf
1887 Edinburgh. [NAS.SC70.1.258]

MCLEAN, ALEXANDER, a brickmaker in Omaha, Nebraska, by
1889, son of Alexander McLean in Dunfermline, Fife, who
died 21 July 1888. [NAS.SH.30.10.1889]

MCLEAN, DONALD, MD, in Detroit, 1892. [NAS.SH.8.4.1892]

MCLEAN, JAMES, a joiner, married Agnes Mill, second daughter
of George Mill in Saddlestone, Angus, in San Mateo,
California, on 16 December 1884. [S#12752]

MCLEAN, L. A., son of Captain McLean of the 93rd (Sutherland)
Highlanders, married Eliza N. Smith, daughter of Colonel
Robert Smith of Edgewood, in Edgewood, Lexington,
Missouri, on 15 February 1849. [SG#1820]

MCLEAN, WILLIAM, born in 1838, youngest son of James
McLean in Wester Baldridge, Fife, settled in the American
South before the Civil War, died in San Francisco on 10
January 1871. [FH]

MACLEAN, ..., daughter of Professor Donald MacLean of the
University of Michigan, was born in Ann Arbor on 20
November 1878. [EC#29393]

MCLEAY, ALEXANDER, farmer in Bottineau, Dakota, by 1891,
son of Alexander McLeay, a laborer in Montrose, Angus,
who died 3 June 1890. [NAS.SH.2.1.1891]

MCLEAY, DONALD, in Portland, Oregon, cnf 1898 Edinburgh.
[NAS.SC70.1.366/161]

MACLEAY, HUGH, (of Lipman and Company), from Golspie,
Sutherland, died in Portland, Oregon, on 3 March 1881.
[S#11,746]

MCLEISH, JOHN, son of John McLeish and Jane Butchart [1789-
1862], settled in California. [Forfar g/s, Angus]

MCLELLAN, GEORGE, born 4 June 1845, eldest son of Peter McLellan, an iron merchant in Glasgow, and Elizabeth Shaw, died in San Francisco on 10 January 1880. [S#11385][MG#2/382]

MACLELLAN, JOHN LATTA, born 9 June 1862, son of Duncan MacLellan and Christine Latta in Glasgow, died in Denver, Colorado, on 6 July1889. [MG#2/381]

MCCLELLAN, ROBERT, born in Annan, Dumfries-shire, on 2 April 1840, son of John Scott McLellan and Isabella Blacklock, married Mary Ann George, in Pennsylvania by 1865, died in Bagley, Iowa, on 4 March 1912. [MG#2/322]

MCLEOD, ANNIE MURRAY, second daughter of Donald McLeod in Anstruther, Fife, married Alfred Squires, in Wichita, Kansas, on 23 May 1890. [EFR]

MCLEOD, THOMAS, in New Baltimore, Michigan, 5 February 1861. [NAS.RS.Edinburgh#77/89]

MCLEOD, THOMAS, married Isabella Patterson, daughter of Alexander Patterson from Bands of Cullen, Banffshire, in Dallas, Texas, on 22 June 1878. [S#10,913]

MCLERAN, JAMES, at Mount Pleasant, Iowa, son of James McLeran, a wright in Dalmellington, who died 5 October 1829. [NAS.SH.18.6.1885]

MACLURE, ALEXANDER, in New Harmony, Indiana, 1840. [NAS.SH.16.7.1840]

MCMASTER, JOHN, in St Louis, Missouri, 1903. [NAS.RS.Wigtown.12.61]

MCMASTER, ROBERT MCKIE, died in Alpena, Michigan, on 13 February 1890. [Wigtown g/s]

MCMASTER, WILLIAM, born 1845, from Glasgow, soldier of the US 7th Cavalry, in 1876. [S]

MCMILLAN, ELIZABETH CORSON, daughter of Robert McMillan and his wife Janet Douglas, from Kiekcudbright, and wife of George B.Shepherd, died in Franklin, St Mary's parish, Louisiana, on 25 September 1882. [S#12,249]

MCMILLAN, ELIZABETH, born in 1854, wife of Robert Sproat late in Lennox Plunton, died on 12 April 1908, buried in Boise, Idaho.[Senwick g/s]

MCMILLAN, ..., born 1799, a clerk, emigrated via Port Glasgow on the Jamaica, master John Heron, bound for New Orleans to settle there, arrived 19 January 1829. [USNA.M259/7]

MCMILLAN,........., daughter of Neil McMillan, was born in Kansas on 8 November 1873. [S#9450]

MCMURTRIE, EPHRAIM, in Chicago, 1886, son of James McMurtrie, Hillhead of Enterkin, Tarbolton, Ayrshire, who died 27 September 1849. [NAS.SH.26.3.1886]

MCMURTRIE, MARGARET, wife of David Berwick in Oaklands, California, died 18 August 1903.
[St Andrews Cathedral g/s, Fife]

MCNAGHTON, MALCOLM M., second son of Finlay McNaghton a merchant in Glasgow, was drowned in the Mississippi River, near St Louis, on 26 April 1843. [SG#1228]

MCNALLY, JOHN, from Paisley, Renfrewshire, died in New Orleans, cnf 1886 Edinburgh. [NAS.SC70.1.251/374]

MACNAUGHTON, JOHN, in Kaukauna, Wisconsin, by 1899. [NAS.SH.19.10.1899]

MCNAUGHTON, MARGARET, daughter of George McNaughton, Woodside, Aberdeen, married Samuel Vial, in Hazelgrove, Illinois, on 19 November 1846; died in Hazel Grove, Illinois, on 18 May 1856. [AJ#5168/5657]

MCNEIL, ARCHIBALD, from Colonsay, sometime Lieutenant Colonel of the Aberdeenshire Fencibles, then HM Consul in Leghorn, late HM Consul in New Orleans, Louisiana, died on way from Canada to New York on 25 September 1808. [NAS.CS17.1.29/4][SM#71/78][NAS.NRAS#GD51.6/1657; 1/580]

MCNEIL, JAMES, son of David McNeil, settled in Bountyful, Davis County, Utah, in 1873, then in St George, Washington County, Utah, in 1879, in Pinal City, Pinal County, Arizona,

1881, then in Globe City, Pinal County, Arizona, in Clifton, Arizona 1883, died in Puma, Graham County, Arizona, 18 March 1884. [StAUL:MS32]

MCNEIL, JOHN, son of David McNeil, emigrated via Liverpool and New York to Smithfield, Utah, in 1870, moved to Davis County, Utah, in 1871, then a miner in Evenstone, Wyoming, moved to Alta City, Little Cottonwood Canyon, Utah, in 1872, late in Rock Spring, Sweetwater County, Utah, in 1886. [StAUL:MS32]

MCNICOL or NICOL, JAMES HUNTER, in California before 1863.[NAS.SH.5.11.1863]

MCOMISH, JOHN, settled in New Orleans, died on 19 August 1830. [NAS.SH]

MCPHERSON, ALEXANDER, grandson of William Beckton in Eaglesfield, died in Cherokee, Iowa, on 2 October 1887. [AO: 25.11.1887]

MCPHERSON, BARBARA, eldest daughter of William McPherson a farmer in Muirton, Forres, Morayshire, married Joseph John Mason, in San Francisco on 14 September 1872. [S#9114]

MCPHERSON, DONALD, a farmer in Kalamazoo, Michigan, who died 20 June 1887, father of Frederick Angus McPherson. [NAS.SH.1.11.1889]

MCPHERSON, JOHN, in Detroit, Michigan, brother of Mary Jane McPherson in Oban, Argyllshire, who died 6 December 1896. [NAS.SH.23.3.1897]

MCPHERSON, M., from Eaglesfield, Dumfries-shire, then in Wheatfield Township, Will County, Indiana, married John Patterson of Union, Indiana, on 19 August 1879. [AO]

MCPHERSON, WILLIAM, born in 1878, son of Donald MacPherson [1827-1900] died in Caldwell, Idaho, on 6 February 1910. [Croick g/s, Ross-shire]

MCPHERSON,......., son of John McPherson, was born in Calestoga, California, on 13 August 1882. [S#12,220]

MCQUAKER, SARAH HERON or, in Henry, Dakota, sister of Jessie Heron, Barrachan, Wigtownshire, who died 19 October 1885. [NAS.SH.12.5.1885]

MCQUEEN, ALEXANDER WILLIAMSON, a plumber in South Minneapolis, Minnesota, by 1891, son of Alexander McQueen in Aberdeen who died 17 April 1891. [NAS.SH.5.8.1891]

MCQUEEN, ISABEL, daughter of George McQueen from Wicketthwaite, Kirkpatrick-Fleming, Dumfries-shire, wife of Robert Rae, died Detroit 13 July 1879. [AO]

MCQUEEN, JAMES, from Dunfermline, Fife, died in Detroit on 9 November 1884.[PJ]

MCQUEEN, JAMES, jr., born in Dunfermline, Fife, during 1854, a railwayman who died in Detroit during 1898. [FFP, 24.9.1898]

MCQUEEN, MAGGIE, eldest daughter of John McQueen a bleacher in Dunfermline, Fife, and wife of John Crichton, died in Towarda, Illinois, on 26 September 1895. [DJ]

MCQUEEN, WILLIAM G., youngest son of James McQueen, died in Detroit on 6 May 1901. [DJ]

MACRITCHIE, JOHN, eldest son of W. D. MacRitchie MD HEICS, married Agnes Leaming, daughter of Hugh Leaming, Butler County, Kansas, in Emporia, Kansas, on 27 September 1873. [EC#27702] [S#9445]; John McRitchie, a farmer in Eldorado, Kansas, 1892. [NAS.SH.11.2.1892]

MACRITCHIE, THOMAS ELDER, born in 1849, third son of W. D. MacRitchie MD, HEICS, 4 Archibald Place, Edinburgh, died at Little Walnut township, Butler County, Kansas, on 7 June 1875. [EC#28311][S#9963]; cnf 10 January 1876 Edinburgh. [NAS.SC70.1.176/469]

MACRITCHIE, WILLIAM, second son of W. D. MacRitchie MD HEICS, married Emma Augusta, daughter of George W. Miller, Butler County, Kansas, in Quito, Kansas, on 19 August 1874. [EC#28063][S#9715]

MCRITCHIE,......., daughter of John McRitchie, was born at twin
Springs, Butler County, Kansas, on 20 October 1874.
[S#9764]

MACRITCHIE, ..., daughter of William MacRitchie, was born at
Little Walnut, Butler County, Kansas, on 14 May 1875.
[EC#28289]

MACRITCHIE, ..., daughter of John MacRitchie, was born in
Glencoe, Butler County, Kansas, on 7 December 1876.
[EC#28788][S#10,436]

MACRITCHIE, ..., daughter of William MacRitchie, was born in
Little Walnut, Kansas, on 21 May 1877. [S#10,577]

MCVICAR, PATRICK, born 1841, son of Reverend J. G. McVicar
in Moffat, Dumfries-shire, died at the Alpin Hotel, Colorado,
18 August 1880. [AO:17.9.1880]

MCVITTIE, ALEXANDER MCLEOD, infant son of Alexander
McVittie, died in Detroit on 3 July 1873. [EC#27719]

MCWHAN, THOMAS, son of James McWhan and Jane Haining, a
merchant in New Orleans before 1848. [NAS.SH]

MCWILLIAMS, JOHN, died in San Francisco in February 1853.
[EEC#22421]

MCWILLIAMS, ROBERT, from Cairnie, Banffshire, emigrated to
Savannah, Ohio, in 1840s, moved to Cedar County, Iowa, in
1851, married Margaret Beveridge and settled as a farmer in
Lincoln, Iowa.[ENES#1.252]

MAIBEN, ROBERT, in Wisconsin, 1855.
[NAS.SC48.49.25.55/151]

MAILER, ANDREW, son of Andrew Mailer a mason in Edinburgh,
settled as a shoemaker in Depere, Wisconsin, before 1877.
[NAS.SH.25.6.1877]

MAIR, JAMES, born in 1832, from Savoch, Aberdeenshire, died at
Lake Shetek, Wisconsin, on 4 February 1875.
[AJ:17.3.1875]

MAITLAND, FORBES, son of Robert Maitland a shipowner in
Aberdeen, died in Los Angeles, California, on 7 August
1874. [AJ:23.9.1874]

MALCOLM, MARGARET ERNESTINE, youngest daughter of
William Malcolm the parochial schoolmaster of Echt,
Aberdeenshire, married George Lillie Center, in Berkeley,
California, on 6 April 1877. [S#10,548]

MALCOLM, ROBERT DOIG, born 1843, son of David Malcolm
and Elspeth Doig, died in Belle Fourche, South Dakota,
during 1909. [Glamis g/s, Angus]

MALLOCH, WILLIAM, in Colorado Springs, cnf 1896 Edinburgh.
[NAS.SC70.1.352]

MANSON, DONALD, born 1798, late of the Hudson Bay Company,
died at Champoeg, Marion County, Oregon, on 7 January
1880. [S#11,450]

MANSUR, ALVAH, in St Louis, Missouri, cnf 1898 Edinburgh.
[NAS.SC70.1.385/829]

MARNOCH, Dr G. F., late of Great King Street, Edinburgh, died in
Texas on 16 August 1870. [S#8466]

MARQUIS, ALEXANDER, son of John Marquis a victualler in
Glasgow, settled in Milwaukee, Wisconsin, before 1881.
[NAS.SH.7.11.1881]

MARR, JOHN, a clerk in Chicago, 1878. [NAS.RS.Forfar.34.255]

MARSHALL, GEORGE, in San Francisco, cnf 1868 Edinburgh.
[NAS.SC70.1.141.295]

MARSHALL, JAMES, from Cramond, Midlothian, died at Sutter's
Creek, California, on 7 October 1874. [S#9771]

MARSHALL, JAMES, born 1837, a joiner and builder, third son of
William Marshall a farmer in South Queensferry, died in
Mmoak, Illinois, on12 August 1881. [S#11,900]

MARSHALL, JOHN, with his wife Elizabeth, settled in Bountyful,
Davis County, Utah, in 1871, moved to Marshallville,
Sessions Settlement, Davis County, in 1872. [StAUL:MS32]

MARSHALL, WALTER, in Chicago, 1887, son of Walter Marshall a spirit dealer in Alva, Stirlingshire, who died 23 August 1866. [NAS.SH.24.11.1887]

MARSHALL, WILLIAM, born in Dundee 1740, son of William Marshall (died 1781) a merchant in Dundee and Christine Pilmore (1720-1751), died in New Orleans on 23 December 1803. [Howff g/s, Dundee]

MARTIN, HELEN, daughter of Mary Bryce or Martin, possibly from Wigtownshire, wife of ..... Nelson, in San Francisco by 1879. [NAS.SH.10.12.1879]

MARTIN, W., arrived in San Francisco from Glasgow on board the barque <u>Madeira</u>, Captain Douglas, on 9 November 1851. [SFL#3/2]

MASON, ROBERT, son of Robert Mason a shoemaker in South Queensferry, West Lothian, settled as a baker in Rockford, Illinois, by 1877.[NAS.SH.10.12.1877]; a baker in Rockford, Illinois, 1878. [NAS.RS.Queensferry.4.262]

MASTERTON, ..., son of John Nevay Masterton, chief clerk at the Quartermaster's Department, US Army, was born at Fort Griffin, Texas, 30 September 1873. [S#9446]

MATHESON, DUNCAN, son of Donald Matheson [died 1875] and Isabella ....[died 1885], settled in Colorado. [Gairloch g/s, Wester Ross]

MATHESON, HECTOR, son of Donald Matheson [died 1875] and Isabella ....[died 1885], settled in Colorado. [Gairloch g/s, Wester Ross]

MATHESON, KENNETH, son of Donald Matheson [died 1875] and Isabella ....[died 1885], settled in Colorado. [Gairloch g/s, Wester Ross]

MATHESON, ROBERT POPE, in Datil, New Mexico, by 1899, son of William James Matheson in Edinburgh who died 17 June 1892, and grandson of Robert Matheson of Coates, an architect in Edinburgh, who died 5 March 1877. [NAS.SH.17.6.1899]

MATTHEWSON, AGNES, born in 1817, widow of William G.
Dobie, died in Kansas City on 27 December 1898.
[Dunfermline g/s, Fife]

MATHEWSON, Dr ROBERT, born in Scotland during 1820, a
mining engineer,settled in California around 1850, died on
30 April 1867. [Alta California, 3.5.1867]

MAXWELL, JOHN, from Annan, Dumfries-shire, died in Chicago
on 21 May 1887. [AO:24.6.1887]

MAY, CHARLES, son of Mrs S. F.May, 12 Panmure Place,
Edinburgh, died in Austin, Texas, on 29 June 1882.
[S#12,183]

MEALL, DEWAR, in New Buttergask, Cawker City, Kansas, 1878.
[NAS.SC48.49.25.78/110]

MEARNS, JOHN SINCLAIR, in San Antonio, Texas, by 1892, son
of William Mearns a shipmaster who died 1 April
1872.[NAS.SH.8.9.1892]

MECOMB, W. H., arrived in San Francisco on 13 July 1851 on
board the William, Captain Gellatly, from Glasgow.
[SFL#1/175]

MEGGET, AGNES, daughter of Thomas Megget, Writer to the
Signet in Edinburgh, died in New Orleans on 8 August 1867.
[S#7512]

MEIKLE, G., arrived in San Francisco on 13 July 1851 on board the
William, Captain Gellatly, from Glasgow. [SFL#1/175]

MEIKLE, ..., daughter of William Meikle, was born in
Indianapolis, Indiana, on 3 December 1877. [S#10,739]

MEIKLEJOHN, MARY ROSS, relict of Robert B. Harkness,
Edinburgh, died at the residence of her brother in law, James
Hutton, in Lanark, Wisconsin, on 11 January 1883.
[S#12,339]

MELDRUM, MARGARET, eldest daughter of William Meldrum a
schoolmaster in Dunfermline, Fife, who died in 1846, and
wife of David Bruce Lothian, eldest son of James Lothian a

printer in Alloa, Clackmannanshire, who died in 1862, died in Chicago on 8 July 1872. [FA][S#9060]

MELDRUM, ..., son of Barclay F. G. Meldrum, was born in Benicia, California, 2 June 1861. [S#1901]

MELLISS, DAVID ERNEST, a civil and mining engineer in San Francisco, by 1890, grand-nephew of Agnes McHaffie who died 24 February 1890. [NAS.SH.31.10.1890]

MELLISS, IDA, in San Francisco, by 1890, grand-nephew of Agnes McHaffie who died 24 February 1890. [NAS.SH.31.10.1890]

MELVILLE, JOHN, in Kensington, Walsh County, Dakota, cnf 1886 Edinburgh. [NAS.SC70.1.254/767]

MELVILLE, MARY MCGREGOR, daughter of George P. Melville, California, married Allen B. Palmer from New York, in Newport, Fife, 14 October 1862. [S#2286]

MELVILLE, WILLIAM, son of Alexander Melville of Hallfield, Fife, (1784-1842) and Grace Babbington (1779-1823), died in Austin, Texas, aged 25. [Dumfries g/s]

MELVIN, ANNIE, daughter of John Melvin, Dunfermline, Fife, married Peter Robertson, Del Norte, Rio Grande, Colorado, in Silverton, San Juan, Colorado, on 6 September 1883. [S#12,547]

MENZIES, ARCHIBALD, born in Weem, Perthshire, surgeon, educated in Edinburgh, served under Captain George Vancouver, RN, as a naval surgeon and botanist during voyages to the Pacific Northwest, 1792-1794

MERCER, JOANNA NEILSON, in Franklin, Oneida County, Idaho, cnf 1897 Edinburgh. [NAS.SC70.1.361]

MERRYLEES, MARY, fifth daughter of William Merrylees in Lerwick, Shetland Islands, married Rev, Oscar Chute of Vineland, New Jersey, at the State Agricultural College, Lansing, Michigan, 23 June 1868. [S#7790]

MILES, THOMAS, born in 1832, son of Thomas Miles and
Margaret Thomson, died at North Fork, American River,
California, on 24 May 1852.[St Andrews g/s, Fife]

MILL, JANE, eldest daughter of George Mill, Monikie, Angus,
married John McLaren, San Mateo, California, at Russ
House, San Francisco, on 31 July 1876. [S#10,327]

MILLANS, THOMAS, son of Thomas Millans, Drumdryan House,
Edinburgh, died in Galveston 1863. [S.12.11.1853]

MILLER, AGNES JANET NICHOLSON, in Columbus, County
Colorado, Texas, cnf 1868 Edinburgh.
[NAS.SC70.1.141.535]

MILLER, ELIZABETH, daughter of George Miller, St
Magdalene's, Perth, married David Walker from Fife, in
Helena, Arkansas, on 25 December 1875. [S#10,144]

MILLER, FREDERICK GEORGE, a clerk in Iowa, youngest son
of James Miller, Springbank, Musselburgh, Midlothian, died
in Emmetsburg, Iowa, on 20 March 1882, [S#12,072]; cnf
1882 Edinburgh. [NAS.SC70.1.218/194]

MILLER, JAMES, in Macomb County, Michigan, 13 December
1848. [NAS.SC37.59.5/156; 12/85]

MILLER, JAMES GRAHAM, second son of John Miller a baker in
Stirling, died in Chicago 9 August 1868. [S#7824]

MILLER, JAMES MUIR, youngest son of William Miller a wood
merchant in Leith, died in Evansville, Indiana, on 23 July
1878. [S#10,951]

MILLER, JAMES SCOTT, a merchant, son of Provost Miller of
Inverkeithing, Fife, died in Washington, Indiana, 19 June
1861. [S#1903]

MILLER, JOHN, died in Columbus, Colorado, on 2 July 1863.
[NAS.SH.1.10.1868]

MILLER, L., arrived in San Francisco from Glasgow on board the
barque Madeira, Captain Douglas, on 9 November 1851.
[SFL#3/2]

MILLER, MAGGIE, daughter of John S. Miller in Annan, Dumfries-shire, married William H, Hutton of Chicago, at 8 Roselyn Place, Chicago, on 2 October 1892. [AO:4.11.1892]

MILLER, MARTHA MAUD, wife of Peter Miller a farmer in Helena, Arkansas, died in Massillon, Ohio, on 1 February 1878. [EC#29144]

MILLER, ROBERT, born 1817, son of David Miller (1776-1824) a brewer and Isabella Gilchrist (1767-1849), died in New Orleans on 6 December 1850. [Howff g/s, Dundee]

MILLER, ROBERT MCLAREN, in Dallas, Texas, grandson of Robert McLaren a skipper in Limekilns who died 17 January 1869. [NAS.SH.12.3.1888]

MILLER, STOCKS, younger son of Walter Millar of Torr-Kedlock, married Margaret Richards, only daughter of H. B. J. Richards, in Spearfish, Dakota, on 3 September 1884. [S#12859]

MILLAR, STOCKS, son of Walter Miller and Sarah Stocks, died in Moorcroft, Wyoming, in August 1890. [Logie g/s]

MILLER, WILLIAM, in California, 11 September 1869. [NAS.RS.Lochmaben,7/60]

MILLER, WILLIAM GILLIES, son of William Miller and Isabella Cowden in Glencaple, settled in Frenton, Clinton County, Illinois, by 1869. [NAS.SH.17.7.1869]

MILLER, WILLIAM, son of William Miller a merchant in Leith, died in Chicago on 26 October 1877. [S#10,709]

MILLER, WILLIAM, Huntley Grove, Illinois, married Jane Milne, eldest daughter of James Milne, 32 Lorne Street, Leith Walk, Edinburgh, in Huntley, Illinois, on 19 September 1884. [S#12868]

MILLER, ..., daughter of Frederick Miller, was born in Los Angeles on 27 April 1875. [EC#28475]

MILLIKEN, or SCOTT, SARAH, in Missouri, 1887, daughter of Thomas Milliken and his wife Rosina McTier in Wallacetown, Ayr. [NAS.SH.26.8.1887]

MILLONS, THOMAS, born in Leith on 24 April 1830, son of
Thomas Millons and Agnes Noble, died in Galveston, Texas,
on 13 October 1853.[Dean g/s, Edinburgh]

MILNE, ALEXANDER, born in Morayshire, died in New Orleans
in 1838. [IC.26.12.1838]

MILNE, ALEXANDER, son of Robert Milne [1832-1904] and
Isabella Henderson [1834-1905] in Hillhead, Caskieben,
Aberdeenshire, settled in Bixbys, Dakota. [Dyce g/s,
Aberdeenshire]

MILNE, ANDREW, born 1789, emigrated to USA in 1806, a
merchant in New Orleans. [1812]

MILNE, DAVID, son of Robert Milne [1832-1904] and Isabella
Henderson [1834-1905] in Hillhead, Caskieben,
Aberdeenshire, settled in Ogden, Dakota. [Dyce g/s,
Aberdeenshire]; at Mountain Post Office, Pembina, Dakota,
1892. [NAS.SH.16.6.1892]

MILNE, JAMES, born 1833, son of William Milne, Greenside,
Edinburgh, died in Koekuk, Iowa, in April 1871. [S#8670]

MILNE, JAMES, from Keithfield, Tarves, Aberdeenshire, died in
New Orleans on 9 February 1872. [AJ:13.3.1872]

MILNE, JANE, eldest daughter of James Milne, 32 Lorne Street,
Leith Walk, Edinburgh, married William Millar of Huntley,
Illnois, there on 19 September 1884. [S#12868]

MILNE, JOSEPH M., youngest son of George Milne a card cutter,
43 St Leonard's Place, Dunfermline, Fife, died in Chicago on
27 February 1891. [PJ]

MILNE, MARY, eldest daughter of William Milne a farmer, married
James Horne Smith of Union City, Indiana, at Parkhill,
Lumphanans, Aberdeenshire, on 31 March 1876. [AJ#6691]

MINTY, WILLIAM, from Ellon, Aberdeenshire, then of Ascension
parish, Louisiana, married Eliza Gordon, youngest daughter
of William Gordon in Belhelvie, in Ellon, Aberdeenshire, 28
July 1849. [AJ#5299]

MITCHELL, ALEXANDER, a clerk from Aberdeenshire,
emigrated to America in 1839, settled in Milwaukee.
[ENES#1.253]

MITCHELL, ANNE, daughter of Captain Andrew Mitchell in
Cupar, Fife, wife of John Johnston in Knox, Illinois, 1837,
1842. [NAS.SC20.34.20.61/3] [NAS.RGS#228/25]

MITCHELL, DAVID, a merchant in Michilmackinac,
1809.[NAS.CS17.1.28/575,593]

MITCHELL, DAVID, in Yamhill County, Oregon, cnf 1874
Edinburgh. [NAS.SC70.1.168/64]

MITCHELL, DONALD, in Blue Canyon, California, cnf 1889
Edinburgh. [NAS.SC70.1.276]

MITCHELL, ELIZABETH, eldest daughter of William Mitchell
from Dundee, a mill proprietor in Detroit, Michigan, married
William T. Smith a miller, third son of William Miller
manager of Stockbridge Mills, Edinburgh, in Detroit on 30
December 1875. [S#10,152]

MITCHELL, ELIZABETH, born 1851, eldest daughter of William
Mitchell a mill proprietor, and wife of William Smith a
miller, died in Detroit, Michigan, on 22 July 1877.
[S#10,644]

MITCHELL, JAMES ALEXANDER, born 1821, only son of
James Mitchell, a Lieutenant of the 68th Infantry, died in
New Orleans on 12 December 1845. [AJ#5115]

MITCHELL, JOHN, son of Alexander Mitchell in Grantown on
Spey, Morayshire, died in San Francisco 19 May 1870.
[S#8389]

MITCHELL, MINA BELL, born in 1892, daughter of John and
Maggie Mitchell,and grand-daughter of Mrs Bell in
Anstruther Wester, Fife, died in Seattle, Washington, on 13
April 1901. [EFR]

MOAR, JONATHAN, son of Jonathan Moar a blacksmith in
Stromness, Orkney, settled on Souvies Island, Oregon, by
1862.[NAS.SH.2.12.1862]

MOIR, GEORGE, possibly from Aberdeenshire, settled as an engineer in Detroit by 1878. [NAS.SH.27.4.1878]

MOFFAT, JOHN, in Skiddy, Morris County, Kansas, 1894. [NAS.RS.Burntisland.14.170]

MOFFAT, THOMAS, son of Thomas Moffat a tanner in Musselburgh, Midlothian, died in Glasgow, Missouri, on 21 July 1846. [EEC#21413]

MOFFATT, ..., son of R. C. Moffatt, was born at 490 Madison Street,Chicago, on 12 March 1876. [AO]

MOFFATT, ..., daughter of R. C. Moffatt, was born at 30 Lexington Avenue, Chicago, during 1878. [AO]

MONEY, WILLIAM, arrived in California in 1843, settled in Los Angeles. [SHR#153/141]

MONTGOMERY, DAVID, son of John Montgomery a draper in Annan, Dumfries-shire, died at Geneva Lake, Wisconsin, on 20 November 1891. [AO:4.12.1891]

MONTGOMERY, JAMES S., in Galveston, second son of James G. Montgomery a bookseller in Dumfries, married Nina Sweeney, only daughter of Franklin Sweeney, Bragoria County, in Quintana, Texas, on 17 December 1872. [S#9192]

MONTGOMERY, ..., son of James Montgomery, was born in Galveston, Texas, on 4 April 1876. [S#10,218]

MONTGOMERY, ..., son of James S. Montgomery a banker, was born in Galveston, Texas, on 22 November 1878. [S#11,047]

MOODIE, WILLIAM, born 1843, from Edinburgh, soldier of A Company, 7th Cavalry, died at the Battle of the Little Big Horn in June 1876. [S]

MOORE, ALEXANDER, born in Penstone, Scotland, in 1846, died in San Francisco on 30 April 1867. [SF Daily Morning Call, 16.5.1881]

MOOR, CLARA, widow of William Scott a builder from Aberdeen, died in Detroit, Michigan, on 5 May 1852. [AJ:2.6.1852]

MOORE, ..., daughter of Rev. T. Verner Moore, was born in Helena, Montana, on 6 August 1883. [S#12,502]

MOOREHEAD, JAMES DUNCAN, born in Glasgow on 26 May 1850, married Maria Susan Gordon in 1876 in Rosita, Colorado, died in Chehalis, Washington, on 25 August 1928. [WSP]

MORE, ROBERT SMITH, born on 18 October 1828, son of Robert Thomas More and Elizabeth Smith, married Rebecca Ann Wright in Steilacoom, Washington, in 1858, settled in Puyallup, Washington, during 1862, died there on 24 February 1904. [WSP]

MORGAN, ROBERT, in California, cnf 1896 Edinburgh. [NAS.SC70.1.354]

MORGAN, WILLIAM, born 9 December 1836, third son of James Morgan [1790-1860] and Clementina Kyd [1805-1881], died in Selma, Arkansas, on 28 February 1876. [Dean g/s, Edinburgh]

MORISON, or TODD, ELIZABETH, in Austin, Minnesota, by 1890, daughter of Joseph Morison in Glasgow who died 15 February 1889. [NAS.SH.31.10.1890]

MORRIS, DAVID, son of Thomas Morris a grocer in Dalry, settled as a smith in Illinois by 1859. [NAS.SH.6.7.1859]

MORRIS, Mrs ELIZABETH, born in Scotland 27 September 1835, married James B. Morris in Belfast during 1851, emigrated to USA in 1857, via Ohio to Kansas, settled in Geary County, Kansas, died there 23 June 1901. [KK.37.1.13]

MORRIS, JAMES B., born in Scotland 20 August 1828, emigrated to USA in 1857, via Ohio to Kansas, settled in Geary County, Kansas, died there 11 September 1893. [KK.37.1.13]

MORRISON, ADAM, fourth son of John Morrison in Edinburgh, died in Watertown, Minnesota, on 25 December 1868. [S#7981]

MORRISON, ANN, born in 1802, widow of John Young from Crossgates, Fife, died in Springfield, Illinois, on 13 April 1891. [PJ]

MORISON, DAVID, a merchant and shipowner from Montrose, wife Elizabeth Mitchell from Aberdeen, settled in New Orleans in 1790, father of James Martin Morrison (1805-1880), he died 1808. [ANY.2.202]

MORRISON, HUNTER, born 1841, eldest son of Hunter Morrison, St Thomas, West Indies, died in Centerville, Shasta County, California, on 17 April 1879. [S#11,180]

MORRISON, JAMES, born in Scotland during 1845, died in San Francisco on 27 January 1895. [SF Morning Call, 16.5.1881]

MORRISON, or STEVENSON, JANET STUART, in Indianapolis, by 1891, daughter of James Morrison, Greenfield, Irvine, Ayrshire, who died 15 May 1888. [NAS.SH.25.6.1891]

MORISON, JEAN, born in 1796, daughter of John Morison a farmer in Stackadale, Turriff, Aberdeenshire, wife of William Moir an engineer, died at Scotch Settlement, Michigan, on 29 July 1841. [AJ#4888]

MORISON, JOHN, son of John Morison a shipmaster in Ross and Cromarty, settled in Chicago by 1874. [NAS.SH.19.6.1874]

MORRISON, JOHN, eldest son of John Morrison, ACS, in Edinburgh, died in Minneapolis, Minnesota, 15 July 1861. [S#1925]

MORRISON, WILLIAM, son of Thomas Morrison in Wester Dalmeny, died in Orange, Texas, on 19 November 1877. [S#10,737]

MORTON, MARGARET, in Chicago, cnf 1872 Edinburgh. [NAS.SC70.1.159/713]

MOSS, EDWARD L., MD, FRCSI, assistant surgeon RN, married Thomasina Mary Dugale, only daughter of Thomas Dugdale of Clara, King's County, Ireland, in San Francisco on 28 March 1873.[EC#27630]

MOWBRAY, MARGARET, possibly from Stirlingshire, wife of John Anderson, settled in Chicago by 1870. [NAS.SH.15.12.1870]

MOWBRAY, Mr....., arrived in San Francisco on 22 February 1852 on board the <u>Hindustan</u>, Captain Pook, from Glasgow. [SFL#3/83]

MOYES, ALEXINA B., daughter of David Moyes a joiner from Edinburgh, married Cyrus Byler of Durham township, in Pontosoc, Hancock county, Illinois, on 29 January 1873. [S#9250]

MOYES, WILLIAM, died in Alameda County, California, on 13 May 1879. [Howff g/s, Dundee]

MUDIE, ROBERT ANDREW, from Glasgow, resident in Chicago, married Lizzie Melcher Beal, second daughter of Josiah Beal of Portsmouth, New Hampshire, there on 19 January 1870. [S#8279]

MUIR, FRANK WILLIAM, infant son of Francis and Ellen Muir, died in San Francisco on 6 November 1870. [S#8530]

MUIR, JAMES, jr., eldest son of James Muir a spirit merchant in Grahamston, Falkirk, Stirlingshire, died in Chicago on 31 January 1873. [S#9235]

MUIR, J. B., in Sheridan, Wyoming, ca.1904. [UGL: UGD91/232]

MUIR, JOHN MCCULLOCH, born in Kirkmabreck on 2 May 1835, son of Reverend John Muir and Gloriana Pearson, died in Denver, Colorado, on 17 March 1899. [F#2.369]

MUIR, PETER, born 1836, son of Peter Muir, Archer's Hall, Edinburgh, died at John Archibald's house in San Francisco on 29 April 1872. [S#8985]

MUIR, THOMAS, a reformer and radical, in Monterey, California, 1796. [NLS.MS3825/6]

MUIR, WILLIAM, in Emmetsburgh, Palo Alto, Iowa, 1890. [NAS.SC48.49.25.89/259]

MUIRHEAD, CATHERINE, daughter of William Muirhead a merchant in Leith, married John Borthwick, in Portland, Oregon, on 18 September 1882. [S#12,248]

MUIRHEAD, KENNETH L., born in Scotland, late master of the British ship Benvenue, died in San Francisco on 17 November 1870. [Alta California, 20.11.1870]

MURISON, ALEXANDER, possibly from Kincardineshire, then in Chicago, died at the Hotel Constanzi, Rome, on 14 March 1876. [S#10,192]

MURISON, JOHN, born in Fraserburgh, Aberdeenshire, in 1816, died in New Orleans on 22 August 1870. [AJ.21.9.1870]

MUNGLE, ALEXANDER, in South Bend, Indiana, son of Alexander Mungle, a farmer in Muirhall, West Calder, who died on 23 November 1876. [NAS.SH.2.3.1897]

MUNNOCH, PETER, son of Peter Munnoch and Margaret Forfar, settled in California by 1898. [Polmont g/s, Stirlingshire]

MUNROE, ALEXANDER H., born in 1845, son of James Munroe [1817-1867] and Mary Hamilton [1820-1848], died in Los Angeles, California, on 27 December 1881. [Crosbie g/s]

MUNRO, ANDREW, born in 1823, son of Andrew Munro and Isabella Urquhart, died in San Francisco, California, on 29 June 1852.[Avoch g/s, Ross and Cromarty]

MUNRO, DONALD, son of David Munro [died in 1890] and Margaret MacDonald [died in 1911], died in Helena, Montana, 12 Nov. 1886. [Kincardine Ardgay g/s]

MUNRO, FREDERICK, a pattern maker, 1491 Chicago Avenue, Chicago, 1908. [NAS.RS.Forfar.73.6]

MURCHESON, JOHN, son of John Murcheson [1779-1867] and Eliza Mackenzie [1786-1877], settled in Sommerville, Union County, Oregon. [Kishorn g/s, Wester Ross]

MURDIE, DAVID, from Jedburgh, Roxburghshire, then in Wabanci, Kansas, died in Topeka, Kansas, cnf 1901 Edinburgh. [NAS.SC70.1.399/271]

MURDOCH, ALEXANDER, son of A. Murdoch and Margaret
Grant, settled in San Francisco by 1873.
[NAS.SH.19.12.1873]

MURDOCH, WILLIAM, son of Allan Murdoch in Catcune Mills,
Gorebridge, died in Chico, California, on 15 April 1876.
[S#10,247]

MURE, JAMES, in California, cnf 1892 Edinburgh.
[NAS.SC70.1.314]

MURE, JOHN, a merchant in New Orleans, married Fanny
Elizabeth Carter, in London on 15 July 1856. [CM#20844]

MURISON, ALEXANDER, from Chicago, died in Rome on 14
March 1876. [EC#28540]

MURPHY, MARY ANN, second daughter of Peter Murphy in
Edinburgh, married Charles Dick Reid, third son of
Alexander Reid from Edinburgh, in Chicago on 25 June
1873. [S#9355]

MURRAY, ALEXANDER, a farmer in Michigan, 1884.
[NAS.SC48.49.25.84/241]

MURRAY, ALEXANDER, in Evanston, Illinois, son of John
Murray a baker in Kinglassie, Fife, who died 20 February
1885. [NAS.SH.4.8.1885]

MURRAY, ANDREW GEORGE, from Edinburgh, married Marcia
Briggs, daughter of Oscar Briggs of Galveston, Texas, in
Salado, Bell County, Texas, on 3 March 1881. [S#11,763]

MURRAY, ANDREW, a partner in the firm of McMahon and
Gilbert merchants in Galveston, Texas, son of Thomas
Murray LL.D. in Edinburgh, died in Galveston on 6
December 1858. [EEC#23311][CM#21623]

MURRAY, CHARLES, born 1811, son of Reverend Andrew
Murray (1754-1844) and Janet Mackay in Auchterderran,
Fife, died in Louisiana 1853. [Auchterderran g/s]

MURRAY, GEORGE FERGUSON, son of John Murray, in Ballus,
Mintlaw, Aberdeenshire, settled as a merchant in Racine,
Wisconsin, by 1868. [NAS.SH.8.8.1868]

MURRAY, GORDON H., possibly from Dumfries-shire, settled in California by 1854. [NAS.SH..8.11.1854]

MURRAY, Mrs HANNAH, wife of William Murray, died on 12 August 1873 in San Francisco. [EC#27745][S#9397]

MURRAY, IAN, Victoria, Ellis County, Kansas, 1873. [NAS.GD302]

MURRAY, JAMES G. D., youngest son of John Murray WS in Edinburgh, died at Salime Pass, Texas, on 26 October 1874. [EC#28133][S#9785]

MURRAY, JANET, only daughter of Captain John Murray from Leith, married Frank M. Darst of Darst, in Eureka, Illinois, on 20 February 1877. [S#10,533]

MURRAY, Captain JOHN, in Eureka, Woodford County, Illinois, second son of John Murray of J. & E. Murray and Co., merchants in Leith, died on 18 September 1875. [EC#28398][S#10064]

MURRAY, Reverend JOHN, son of the late Captain John Murray of Eureka, Illinois, born in Leith, married Saide S. Rue, daughter of Alfred Ruse in Cranbury, US, there on 6 September 1876. [S#10,372]

MURRAY, JOHN, in Franklin, Nebraska, 1888, nephew of Susan Murray in Minnigaff, Wigtownshire, who died 3 January 1887. [NAS.SH.16.1.1888]

MURRAY, ROBERT, born in 1844, from Aberdeen, died in Wamego, Kansas, on 26 April 1874. [AJ:20.5.1874]

MURRAY, WILLIAM, probably from Dumfries-shire, settled as a farmer in Wisconsin by 1869. [NAS.SH.1.5.1869]

MURRAY, WILLIAM, born in Cummertrees, Dumfries-shire, during 1820, nephew of James Landwell a farmer in Priesthill, died in St Louis, Missouri, on 12 November 1871. [AO]

MURRAY, WILLIAM, born in 1825, son of William Murray, Springbank Terrace, Aberdeen, died in Louisville, Kentucky, on 15 November 1852.[AJ:8.12.1852]

MURRAY, ..., son of Andrew Murray, late of Blandfield House, Edinburgh, then a merchant in Galveston, Texas, was born in Corpus Christi on 2 January 1859. [CM#21657]

MURRAY,......, son of Andrew George Murray from Edinburgh, was born in Salado, Texas, on 7 March 1882. [S#12,076]

MURRAY, ..., daughter of Andrew G. Murray, was born in Belton, Texas, on 9 November 1883. [S#12,601]

MYLES, ELIZA GREIG, eldest daughter of Robert Myles, Dalgairn, Cupar, Fife, married John Honeyman, Emerson, Iowa, in Chicago on 14 June 1873. [S#9347]

MYLES, ELIZA CRAIG, born in 1848, daughter of Robert Myles and Helen Cellars, died in Emerson, Mills County, Iowa, on 15 May 1874. [Cupar, Fife, g/s]

NAIRN, JAMES EDMONDSTONE, an engineer, Huntley Grange, Minnesota, 1886. [NAS.SH.5.7.1886]

NEIL, JAMES L., born in 1849, son-in-law of Hugh M. Thomson of Long Grove, Scott County, Iowa, died in Davenport, Iowa, on 11 October 1878. [AO]

NEILSEN, CARL STEFFANSON, in Harshaw, Arizona, by 1890, son of Carl Neilsen, a shipbroker, and Janet Wright (died February 1863) in Dundee. [NAS.SH.23.10.1890]

NEILSON, DANIEL CUMMING, son of Alexander Neilson a writer in Port Glasgow, died in San Francisco on 7 January 1874. [EC#27881][S#9533]

NELSON, ANNIE, daughter of Fairley Nelson, and sister to to W. B. Nelson rector of Musselburgh Grammar School, died in San Francisco on 6 July 1879. [S#11,247]

NICHOLSON, AGNES JANET, died in Columbus, Colorado, on 9 February 1857. [NAS.SH.1.10.1868]

NICHOLSON, DAVID, in Indianapolis, 22 April 1865.

[NAS.RS.Lochmaben#6/119]

NICHOLSON, MALCOLM, of the firm of Sir J. Hobson and Company of New Orleans, died there on 11 June 1833. [SG.2.160][SG#164]

NICHOLSON, SAMUEL, born in Williamsfield, Dumfries-shire, died in Williams Park, Clear Water, Minnesota, on 8 November 1869. [AO]

NICHOLSON, WILLIAM, in Middleton, California, grandson of William Nicholson a blacksmith in Holmshaw who died 20 March 1884. [NAS.SH.12.11.1886]

NICHOLSON, ..., son of James B. Nicholson, was born at Hillside, Le Mars, Iowa, in 1885. [AO: 4.12.1885]

NICHOLSON, ..., daughter of James B. Nicholson, was born at Hillside, Iowa, on 5 November 1887.[AO: 23.12.1887]

NICHOLSON, ..., son of James B. Nicholson, was born at Hillside, Iowa, on 12 December 1889. [AO: 3.1.1890]

NICOL, JANET, daughter of Andrew Nicol a farmer in Cleughhead, wife of Martin Jefferson in Ownes, Illinois, 1867. [NAS.SH.22.1.1867]

NICOL, WALTER, settled in St Helen's parish, Louisiana, married Jane Harvey in Springfield, Livingston parish in 1821, a timber executive in New Orleans, died in 1861. [Walter Nicol's Diary, University of North Carolina]

NICOL,...., son of James Nicol, was born in Baton Rouge, Louisiana, on 24 September 1841. [AJ#4896]

NICOLL, DAVID, born on 3 May 1847, son of James and Jane Nicoll, a shipmaster who died in Port Townsend, Washington, on 14 January 1897. [Monifieth g/s, Angus]

NICOLSON, JANET, born 1851, daughter of David Nicolson and Jacobina Moore, died in Parkside, Chicago, on 27 March 1893. [Bower g/s, Caithness]

NISBET, ELIZABETH ISABELLA, possibly from Edinburgh, wife of Andrew Fraser in Illinois, 1863. [NAS.SH.7.5.1863]

NISBET, JOHN, eldest son of William Nisbet in Ladybank, Ayrshire, died in Willow Valley, Greenwood County, Kansas, on 30 October 1879.[EC#29689]

NISBET, W.C., born 1856, a clerk, youngest son of William Nisbet bootmaker in David Street, Edinburgh, died in Montana on 25 May 1882. [S#12,146]

NIVEN, JOHN, late of St Monance, Fife, died in Urbanna, Illinois, on 30 December 1873. [S#9510]

NIVEN, WILLIAM, in Anaconda, Montana, cnf 1895 Edinburgh. [NAS.SC70.1.345]

NOBLE, ELIZABETH BLAIKIE eldest daughter of David Noble from Edinburgh, married W. S. Mitchell, in Kansas City on 12 November 1870. [S#8533]

NORVAL, JAMES, an ironfounder in Davenport, Iowa, died in 1835. [NAS.SH.30.11.1882]

OGILVIE, ADAM G., born in Keith, Banffshire, 1804, married Isabella Milne, settled in Muscatine County, Iowa, by 1836, died 5 February 1865, buried in Greenwood Cemetery, Muscadine. [IGS/HH.33.3.169]

OGILVIE, DAVID, in Detroit, Michigan, by 1896, nephew of Davina Munro in Forres, Morayshire, who died 28 September 1878. [NAS.SH.15.5.1896]

OGILVY, DAVID GRAHAM DRUMMOND, Earl of Airlie, died in Denver, Colorado, 25 September 1881, cnf 5 January 1882 Forfar.

OGILVIE,......., daughter of Captain S. Ogilvie, was born in San Francisco on 6 October 1877. [S#10,701]

OLIPHANT, ANN HAY, in Colorado, cnf 1892 Edinburgh. [NAS.SC70.1.306]

OLIPHANT, ALEXANDER COLVILLE, second son of Major Oliphant of Over Kinneddar, Fife, drowned near Austin, Texas, on 7 May 1882. [S#12,118]

OLIVER, GLADYS JEMIMA, infant daughter of William and Lizzie Oliver, died in Virginia City, Nevada, on 4 April 1882. [AO:4.5.1882]

OLIVER, HARRY, son of William H. Oliver, died in Virginia City, Nevada, on 7 December 1891. [AO:11.12.1891]

OLIVER, ROBERT, born 15 December 1889, son of William H. Oliver, died in Virginia City, Nevada, on 7 August 1890. [AO:15.8.1890]

OLIVER, WILLIAM H., of De Soto County, Kansas, married Lizzie Moore of Westport, Missouri, there in 1871. [AO]

OLIVER, WILLIAM H., born 1832, died in Virginia City, Nevada, on 5 November 1894. [AO:7.12.1894]

OLIVER, ..., daughter of W. H. Oliver, was born in Westport, Missouri, on 13 July 1873. [AO]

OLIVER, ..., daughter of W. H. Oliver, was born in Virginia City, Nevada, on 29 April 1876. [AO]

OLIVER, ..., son of W. H. Oliver, was born in Virginia City, Nevada, on 20 June 1880. [AO:16.7.1880]

ORMISTON, JANE, wife of William F. Blackhall, died in Des Moines, Iowa, on 4 March 1883, buried in Cockburnspath, Berwickshire on 9 April 1883. [S#12,397]

OSBURNE, ESTHER, born in 1846, daughter of William Osburne of Abbeytown, Dumfries-shire, and wife of Richard Pearson of Cowthwaite, Dumfries-shire, died in Platteville, Nebraska, on 14 June 1872. [AO]

OUTERSON, ..., son of T. S. Outerson a joiner, was born in Marquette, Michigan, on 10 July 1883. [S#12,498]

OVENS, JAMES, in Somerset, Nebraska, by 1899, son of Thomas Ovens in Setonfield, Cockenzie, East Lothian, and his wife Eleanor Kennedy Crawford who died 13 November 1895. [NAS.SH.12.1899]

OWEN, Reverend HENRY JAMES, born 1845, son of Reverend Joseph Owen of the American Presbyterian Mission in

Allahbad, India, died at Colorado Springs, Colorado, on 31 March 1878. [S#10,846]

PAISLEY, ANDREW, born 1801, died in Brockway, St Clair, Michigan, on 2 November 1886. [AO:17.12.1886]

PALMER, ROBERT, born 1833, son of James Palmer, schoolmaster of Kirkurd, Peebles-shire, died in a railway accident in Little Rock, Arkansas, on 21 October 1884. [S#12896]

PANKHURST, ..., daughter of Reverend M. M. Pankhurst, was born at 1238 Michigan Avenue, Chicago, on 16 July 1875. [S#9994]

PANKHURST, ..., son of Reverend M. M. Pankhurst, was born at 218 Dearborn Avenue, Chicago, on 15 March 1879. [S#11,141]

PARK, WILLIAM, died in Thornville, Michigan, 6 April 1861, father of William Wishart Park. [NAS.SH.16.12.1890]

PARK, WILLIAM L., from Dumfries-shire, married Agnes B. Gillespie from Dumfries-shire, in Chicago during 1867. [AO]

PARKER, HENRY, in San Quentin, California, by 1896, son of James Parker, probably from King Street, Calton, Glasgow, a shipping agent in San Francisco who died 28 June 1859. [NAS.SH.16.9.1896]

PARKER, JAMES, probably from King Street, Calton, Glasgow, a shipping agent in San Francisco who died 28 June 1859. [NAS.SH.16.9.1896]

PARKER, JAMES, died in San Quentin, California, on 2 January 1878, son of James Parker, probably from King Street, Calton, Glasgow, a shipping agent in San Francisco who died 28 June 1859. [NAS.SH.16.9.1896]

PATON, DAVID BRAID, son of John Paton in Coaltown of Balgonie, Markinch, Fife, died in Detroit, on 11 June 1862. [S#2207]

PATTON, EDWARD, eighth son of Robert Patton a solicitor in Kirkwall, Orkney Islands, died in San Francisco on 16 December 1877. [S#10,765]

PATON, FRANCIS, in Pueblo, Colorado, 1881. [NAS.SC49.48.25.81/256]

PATON, GEORGE, born 1819, died in Detroit on 20 July 1849. [SG.18/1841]

PATON, JOHN, in Lodi, Wisconsin, by 1881. [NAS.SH.16.2.1881]

PATON, WILLIAM, born in Lanarkshire during 1799, died in Detroit, Michigan, on 17 August 1849, his wife Christine born in Lanarkshire around 1783, died in Detroit on 7 August 1849, Samuel Paton born in 1826, died on 7 August 1849, George Paton born in 1810, died on 8 August 1849, and Jane Paton born in 1823, died on 9 August 1849. [SG#1861]

PATTEN, HENRY TOWER, possibly from Greenock, in Denver, Colorado, by 1891. [NAS.SH.23.6.1891]

PATTERSON, ARCHIBALD, a farmer in Santa Clara, California, by 1868.[NAS.SH.25.6.1868]

PATTERSON, ELIZABETH, born 1780, daughter of John Patterson [1747-1831] and Jean Tweedie [1742-1821], died at Long Grove, Iowa, 2 December 1866. [West Linton g/s, Peeblesshire]

PATTERSON, ISABELLA, eldest daughter of Alexander Patterson, Bands of Cullen, Banffshire, married Thomas McLeod, in Dallas, Texas, on 22 June 1878. [S#10,913]

PATTERSON, JAMES, in San Francisco, son of John Paterson [1783-1874] and Agnes Colville [1787-1844]. [Ochiltree g/s, Ayrshire]

PATERSON, JAMES, from Aberdeenshire, settled in Ashland County, Ohio, moved to Iowa in 1853. [ENES#1.252]

PATTERSON, JESSIE, born in 1830, wife of James Rossie, died in Topeka, Kansas, on 24 February 1905. [Dunning g/s, Perthshire]

PATERSON, SALLIE, wife of Edward Kerr, died at 9 Glen Park Avenue, San Francisco, on 21 September 1883. [S#12,579]

PATTERSON, THOMAS, third son of John Patterson in Kiltehead, Middlebie, Dumfries-shire, died in East Wheatland, Will County, Illinois, on 28 November 1878. [AO]

PAUL, JAMES, second son of John Paul of Newseat, Peterhead, Aberdeenshire, died in Semple, Grant County, Wisconsin Territory, 16 August 1839. [AJ#4786]

PAUL, JOHN, a merchant in Grant County, Wisconsin, married Barbara Gordon, youngest daughter of James Gordon from Edinburgh, in La Crosse, Wisconsin, on 21 May 1863. [S#2494]

PAUL, JOHN FINLAY, born in Ayr 1822, sometime in Glasgow, resident in New Orleans for 30 years, died there on 24 October 1877. [S#10,708]

PAXTON, JOHN, from Edinburgh, died in Moscow, Michigan, 4 October 1861. [S#1983]

PEDDIE, ALEXANDER, son of Alexander Peddie MD in Edinburgh, married Josephine Roper, fourth daughter of Francis H. Roper in Algina, Kossuth County, Iowa, there on 21 October 1875. [EC#28423][S#10075]

PEDDIE, ELIZABETH, only daughter of John Peddie from Montrose, Angus, married William W. Stephens, Spring Valley, youngest son of J. Stephens formerly in Montrose, at the International Hotel, Toano, Nevada, on 16 December 1873. [S#9503]

PEDDIE, JOAN, born 1844, daughter of William Peddie [1821-1884] and Agnes Imrie [1820-1844], died in La Cros, Wisconsin 13 July 1916. [Greyfriars g/s, Perth]

PEDDIE, MARGARET JOSINE, daughter of Alexander Peddie, was born in Emmetsburg, Iowa, on 22 August 1877, died there on 16 March 1882. [S#10,654/12,068] [EC#29002]

PEDDIE, ..., daughter of Alexander Peddie, was born in Emmetsburg, Iowa, on 29 September 1878. [S#10,999]

PEDDIE, ..., daughter of Alexander Peddie, was born in Emmetsburg, Iowa, on 10 February 1883. [S#12,361]

PEEBLES, AGNES, second daughter of Captain Philip Peebles in Pittenweem, Fife, wife of Robert Lawrie, died in Sterling, Illinois, on 1 July 1881. [S#11,859]

PEEBLES, JOHN, a blacksmith, settled in Milwaukee, Wisconsin Territory, by 1847. [OGS.36.1.32]

PEEBLES, WILLIAM, son of Charles Peebles a writer in Glasgow, settled in San Francisco by 1864. [NAS.SH.17.8.1864]

PENMAN, ROBERT PATTERSON, in Fort Wayne, Allan County, Indiana, cnf Edinburgh 1899. [NAS.SC70.1.382/110]

PENNYCOOK, ROBERT, born 1819, from Edinburgh, died in Detroit on 11 June 1872. [S#9031]

PERRY, JAMES, MD, died in Jerseyville, Illinois, on 18 May 1859.[NAS.SH.16.12.1878]

PETER, MARY ANNE, daughter of Thomas H. Peter from Kirkland, Fife, married James Rutherford Carmichael, in Ocheydan, Iowa, on 9 July 1882. [S#12,199]

PHILIP, JESSIE, wife of Neil McMillan, in Victoria, Ellis County, Kansas, 1880. [NAS.PS3.17.51]

PHILP, JOHN, sr., in Nashville, Lee County, Iowa, cnf 1885 Edinburgh. [NAS.SC70.1.242/769]

PILLANS, WILLIAM, born in Howgill Annan, Dumfries-shire, died in Chicago on 1 October 1897. [AO: 5.11.1897]

PIRIE, Mrs ISOBEL, born in 1820, daughter of John Yule, Burnside of Craigievar, Aberdeenshire, died in Red Oak Grove, Cedar County, Iowa, on 11 December 1862. [AJ:14.1.1863]

PITT, WILLIAM, born in 1848, son of William Pitt, a wright [1812-1884], and Isabella Green [1813-1858], died at Copper's Cove, Texas, on 18 September 1882. [Stair g/s, Ayrshire]

PLATT, MARY, born 1852, late of Saughtrees, Wamphrey, Dumfries-shire, wife of David Auston, died at 317 Lincoln Avenue, Chicago, 2 March 1889. [AO: 22.3.1889]

POLLOCK, GEORGE, jr., from Annan, Dumfries-shire, married Alathea M. Lambert of castle Moat, at Castle Meagher County, Montana, on 28 November 1897. [AO:25.2.1898]

PORTEOUS, THOMAS CLARK, born 19 January 1841, settled in New Orleans by 1875, married Octavia Augusta Jones (1852-1882), died in New Orleans on 19 November 1919. [Metrairie g/s, New Orleans]

PORTEOUS, ..., son of W. M. Porteous, was born in St Louis, Missouri, on 16 July 1884. [S#12808]

POTTER, JAMES, in Kansas, cnf 1876 Edinburgh. [NAS.SC70.1.180/480]

POTTS, ANDREW, formerly a book-keeper in Edinburgh, then with the American Fur Company, died at Fort Mackenzie, Upper Missouri, on 25 February 1842. [EEC#20517]

PRENTISE, AGNES, wife of Thomas P. Dick, Rosebank, Robbinsville, Red River, Texas, died on 22 June 1876. [S#10,297]

PRIMROSE, JOHN WILSON, in South Minneapolis, Minnesota, nephew of Sarah Primrose in Edinburgh who died around 1840. [NAS.SH.3.10.1887]

PRINGLE, WILLIAM WATSON, brother of John Pringle of the Scottish Implement Depot in Edinburgh, died in Chicago on 24 August 1873. [EC#27754][S#9406]

PROFIT, CHARLES, from Dundee, settled in New Orleans by 1805. [NAS.CS17.1.24E/161]

PULLAR, ANNIE G., in Summit, Pike County, Missouri, 1871. [NAS.SC49.48.25.71/129]

PURVES, GEORGE, from Dunbar, East Lothian, later in Pine Bluff, Arkansas, cnf Edinburgh 1900. [NAS.SC70.1.388/660]

PURVES, JAMES, a farmer in Lake County, California, cnf 1888 Edinburgh. [NAS.SC70.1.267]

RAE, ANN BELL, born in 1844, died in Dow City, Iowa, on 26 June 1888. [Kettle, Fife, g/s]

RAE, GEORGE JAMES, born 1844, eldest son of Robert Rae in Michigan but from Wickethorn, Kilpatrick-Fleming, Fumfries-shire, died in Shreveport, Louisiana, on 15 September 1873. [AO]

RAE, GEORGE MACAULAY, in Missouri, cnf 1877 Edinburgh. [NAS.SC70.1.186/640]

RAE, GEORGE, son of Thomas Rae a weaver in Kettlebridge, Fife, settled in Dow City, Iowa, by 1883. [NAS.SH.13.9.1883]

RAE, ISOBELLA, born in 1855, daughter of Thomas Rae and Janet Bell, died in Dow City, Iowa, in March 1888. [Kettle, Fife, g/s]

RAE, JESSIE, daughter of James Rae, died in California on 16 January 1901. [Preston g/s, Berwickshire]

RAE, JOHN, born in Aberdeen on 1 June 1796, son of John Rae and Margaret Cuthbert, educated at Marischal College, Aberdeen, arrived in California in 1848, schoolmaster at Sutter's Creek from 1849 to 1851, died in New York on 14 July 1872. [WWW/500]

RAE, ROBERT, married Margaret, eldest daughter of Joseph Harley a cabinetmaker in Buccleuch Street, Edinburgh, in San Francisco on 3 November 1869. [S#8235]

RAE, WALTER B., died in Chester, Illinois, on 10 October 1870. [S#8519]

RAE, WILLIAM GLEN, born in Stromness, Orkney, during 1809 [1812?], son of John Rae in Wyre, Orkney, a Hudson Bay Company employee from 1827 to 1845, arrived at Yerba Buena, San Francisco, in 1841, died in San Francisco on 19 January 1845 [8?]. [W#619] [HBRS#4.355][SHR#153/144]; probate June 1849 PCC

RAEBURN, ..., infant son of John Raeburn and Bella McKerrow, grandson of Thomas Jardine, gardener in Townfoot, Lockerbie, Dumfries-shire, died in Arkansas, Bee County, Texas, 17 February 1878. [AO]

RAINSFORD, Major JOHN C., married Mary, youngest daughter of Richard Lester, Belle Plaine, in Helena, Montana, on 24 November 1873. [EC#277853]

RAMAGE, JOHN CHARLES, son of William Walker Ramage, was born in Central City, Colorado, on 4 September 1875. [S#10038]

RAMSAY, ANNIE, born 1825, widow of John Brown a cattle dealer in Edinburgh, died in Chicago on 9 February 1883. [S#12,362]

RAMSAY, EUPHEMIA, late of Morningside, Edinburgh, wife of James Nielson, died in Detroit, Michigan, on 27 December 1870, mother of a son born 20 December 1870. [S#8575]

RAMSAY, JAMES, born 1779, emigrated to USA in 1802, a merchant in Charleston then in New Orleans, [1812]

RAMSAY, MARGARET, wife of William Peat, daughter of David Ramsay a publisher of the Edinburgh Evening Courant, died in Packwaukie, Wisconsin, in 1877.[EC#28801] [S#10,453]

RATE, GEORGE, in Portland, Oregon, cnf 1895 Edinburgh. [NAS.SC70.1.337]

RAWLINS, Mrs CHARLOTTE, born in 1847, daughter of William Skene from Banchory-Ternan, Kincardineshire, died in Pleasant Valley, Davies County, Illinois, on 14 February 1876.[AJ:22.3.1876]

READ, ISABELLA BARLAND, daughter of Charles Read a bleacher in Roslin, Midlothian, wife of Alexander Bain, died in Stanwood, Iowa, on 2 February 1876. [EC#288513][S#10,165]

REED, JAMES, eldest son of James Reed, MD, in Kilmarnock, Ayrshire, died in New Orleans on 18 September 1839. [SG#8/821]

READMAN, JAMES, in Seattle, 1884. [NAS.NRAS.1219/1]

REID, CHARLES DICK, third son of Alexander Reid in Edinburgh, married Mary Ann Murphy, second daughter of Peter Murphy in Edinburgh, in Chicago on 25 June 1873. [S#9355]

REID, DONALD, son of Catherine Reid in Invergordon, Ross and Cromarty, settled in Denver, Colorado, by 1882. [NAS.SH.8.8.1882]

REID, HELEN, in Texas, 1858. [NAS.SH.27.10.1858]

REID, HUGH, from Cardross, Dunbartonshire, a merchant at Rancho Santa Amita, California, by 1840. [SHR#153/139]

REID, JAMES, at Middle River farm, Minnesota, 1887. [NAS.RS.Forfar.46/49]

REID, WALTER B., son of Alexander Reid, 40 Tower Street, Portobello, died in Chicago on 2 March 1883. [S#12,382]

REID, ..., son of Charles Reid from Edinburgh, was born at Oakley Avenue, Chicago, on 19 October 1874. [S#9761]

RENNIE, HARRIET JANE, wife of Thomas Darling, died in Leadville, Colorado, on 18 October 1879. [S#11,333]

RENWICK, JAMES, married Elizabeth Lockerby, father of William, settled in Davenport, Iowa, died 4 December 1878. [NAS.SH.30.11.1882]

RENWICK, JOHN, born in 1827, son of Walter Renwick from Cleughbrae, Johnston, Dumfries-shire, died at Lodi Station, Illinois, on 9 January 1862. [AO]

RIACH, JOHN JAMES, son of Reverend James Riach in Clither, a farmer in Emmetsburg, Iowa, by 1882. [NAS.SH.30.6.1882]

RICHARDSON, ALEXANDER, late silk mercer in Edinburgh, died in Catfish Prairie, Wisconsin, 1852. [S.16.2.1853]

RICHARDSON, D., in Denver, Colorado, 28 April 1890. [NAS.RS.Lochmaben#10/105]

RICHARDSON, HENRY, born 1827, from Brydekirk Village, Dumfries-shire, died in Tamerack, Illinois, on 10 December 1888. [AO: 4.1.1889]

RICHARDSON, ISABELLA, eldest daughter of D. B. Richardson, Haregills, Ecclefechan, Dumfries-shire, married John Kennedy of Deevale Ranch, Fort McKavitt, Minard County, Texas, in Austin, Texas, on 28 October 1885. [AO:20.11.1885]

RICHARDSON, JOHN, born in 1815, from Hightae, Lochmaben, Dumfries-shire, died in San Francisco on 26 November 1862. [AO]

RICHARDSON, ROBERT, born in 1822, a stonecutter from Hightae, Annandale, Dumfriesshire, died in San Francisco on 6 June 1861.[AO]

RICHARDSON, SUSAN, born in 1810, wife of David Gillespie, from Highlaw, Lockerbie, Dumfries-shire, died at 418 West Madison Street, Chicago, on 27 August 1876. [AO]

RICKARD, WILLIAM, in Texas, cnf Edinburgh 1901. [NAS.SC70.1.407/766]

RIDDLER, JOHN JAMIESON, son of John Riddler a gardener in Aberdeen, settled in Illinois by 1850. [NAS.SH.4.12.1850]

RIDPATH, WILLIAM, eldest son of John Ridpath classics master at Heriot's Hospital, die at Moose Lake, Minnesota, on 15 April 1884. [S#12,719]

RITCHIE, ALEXANDER DALRYMPLE, in Seward, Nebraska, 1887, son of Jane Thomson or Veitch or Ritchie in Edinburgh who died 9 November 1847. [NAS.SH.9.5.1887]

RITCHIE, ANDREW, youngest son of John Ritchie a farmer in Burkshawhead Kirkpatirck-Fleming, Dumfries-shire, died in Green Knowe, McLean County, Illinois, on 12 October 1870. [AO]

RITCHIE, Captain DAVID, master of the <u>William Watson</u>, died at San Francisco Harbor on 24 April 1852. [SFL#3/236]

RITCHIE, HELEN BELL, daughter of James Ritchie of howgillside, Kirkpatrick Fleming, Dumfries-shire, died in Dallflower, Illinois, on 30 August 1869.[AO]

RITCHIE, ISABELLA A., second daughter of Alexander Ritchie in Bishopmill, Elgin, Morayshire, married Andrew Dunsire, born in Buckhaven, Fife, but late from Glasgow, in Missoula, Montana, on 27 May 1892. [FFP]

RITCHIE, JAMES, born 13 January 1820, a merchant in San Francisco, died in Ayr 27 May 1871. [Wallacetown g/s, Ayr][S#8686]

RITCHIE, JAMES ANDREW, third son of Reverend William Ritchie in Longforgan, Perthshire, died in Chicago on 11 July 1879. [EC#29589]

RITCHIE, JOHN, born 1810, a farmer from Birkshawhead, Kilpatrick Fleming, Dumfries-shire, died in Howard, Champaign County, Illinois, on 14 October 1881. [AO:18.11.1881]

RITCHIE, MARGARET, born 1839, daughter of David Ritchie in Largo, Fife, wife of David Ireland in Amherstburg, Canada, died in Detroit, Michigan, on 24 April 1884. [S#12,741]

RITCHIE, MARY GORDON, daughter of John Ritchie, High Street, Kirkcudbright, married James Candlish, from Kirkcudbright, in Eureka, Nevada, on 4 November 1882. [S#12,292]

RITCHIE, Reverend WILLIAM, D.D., from Longforgan, Perthshire, died in Chicago on 11 July 1879. [S#11,241]

ROACH, Mr..., arrived in San Francisco on 22 February 1852 on board the Hindustan, Captain Pook, from Glasgow. [SFL#3/83]

ROBB, JESSIE, eldest daughter of Walter Robb in Inveresk, Musselburgh, Midlothian, married Robert Barrie from Leith, in Detroit 26 June 1871. [S#8724]

ROBERTS, JAMES, born 1794, from Galashiels, Roxburghshire, died in San Francisco, California, on 16 May 1881. [S#11,823]

ROBERTS, ..., son of Charles Roberts, was born in San Francisco on 17 July 1868. [S#7816]

ROBERTS, ..., daughter of John S. Roberts from Galashiels, Roxburghshire, was born at Clark Ranch, Healdsburgh, California, on 10 September 1871. [S#8797]

ROBERTS, ..., son of Charles Roberts, was born in San Francisco on 26 October 1869. [S#8211]

ROBERTSON, AGNES, youngest daughter of John Robertson a feuar in Townhill, Dunfermline, Fife, married James Thompson from Fontanet Vigo, Indiana, at Mount Olive, Illinois, on 9 June 1888. [DJ]

ROBERTSON, DANIEL, son of John Robertson a weaver in Paisley, Renfrewshire, settled in San Francisco by 1876. [NAS.SH.3.6.1876]

ROBERTSON, DAVID, born in 1821, son of George Robertson [1793-1865] and Maria Esther Ireland [1797-1844], died in Sacramento City, California, on 29 June 1850. [Eastern Necropolis g/s, Dundee]

ROBERTSON, DAVID, son of Reverend Patrick Robertson, from Craigdam and Culsalmond, Aberdeenshire, died in St Louis, Missouri, on 31 January 1867. [AJ:27.2.1867]

ROBERTSON, DAVID, eldest son of John Robertson, a joiner in Rigg of Gretna, married Helen Amstrong, youngest daughter of the late George Armstrong, both from Dumfries-shire, married at Fairfax Vicarage, Linn County, Iowa, on 28 September 1888. [AO: 19.10.1888]

ROBERTSON, DUNCAN ENEAS, born in Rochine, son of Charles Robertson and Jean Rose, married Maria Badon from New Orleans, in Louisiana on 7 March 1797. [LGS]

ROBERTSON, DUNCAN, youngest son of Duncan Robertson, wine and spirit merchant, 100 Cowgate, Edinburgh, died in San Francisco on 16 May 1872. [S#8963]

ROBERTSON, ELIZABETH, wife of John Grieve a blacksmith late of Johnston Hall, Middlebie, Dumfries-shire, died in

Long Grove, Scott County, Iowa, on 28 September 1865.
[AO]

ROBERTSON, EUPHEMIA, from Aberdeen, wife of Robert
Gourley, Bon Accord Farm, Michigan, died in St Louis
during June 1852. [AJ: 14.7.1852]

ROBERTSON, FREDERICK WILLIAM, in Waterloo, Iowa,
1877. [NAS.SH.19.9.1877]

ROBERTSON, GEORGE S., late Adjutant of the 51st Light
Infantry, married Eunice Stillwell, eldest daughter of T.
Stillwell of Cuba, Missouri, there on 12 April 1871.
[S#8667]

ROBERTSON, GEORGE, 620 Woodridge Street, West Detroit, 3
March 1880. [NAS.RS.Edinburgh#137/285]

ROBERTSON, GEORGE, from Edinburgh, settled in Detroit,
Michigan, by 1880.[NAS.SH.27.1.1880]

ROBERTSON, HOPE FLEMING, second son of John Robertson
farmer in Laigh of Cluny, Strathtay, Perthshire, died in St
Louis on 28 January 1883. [S#12,362]

ROBERTSON, HUGH, of Crookston, Minnesota, eldest son of John
Robertson from Bothwell Park, Bothwell, Lanarkshire,
married Jessie Jardine McEachran, second daughter of Neil
McEachran, Gleneden, Bothwell, in New York on 29 August
1883. [S#12,523]

ROBERTSON, JANET, daughter of ..... Robertson and Elizabeth
Wilson in Middleton, settled in Wisconsin by 1852.
[NAS.SH.8.4.1852]

ROBERTSON, JOHN, a teacher in Washington 1844.
[NAS.GD16/49/53]

ROBERTSON, JOHN, son of Johnstone Robertson a watchman at
the Govan Silk Factory Glasgow, settled in Belton, Bell
County, Texas, by 1867. [NAS.SH.13.6.1867]

ROBERTSON, JOHN, son of John Robertson a gardener in Govan,
Glasgow, settled as a joiner in San Francisco by 1878.
[NAS.SH.3.8.1878]

ROBERTSON, Reverend JOHN, son of John Robertson of Foveran, Aberdeenshire, died in St Paul, Minnesota, in 1861. [AJ: 31.7.1861]

ROBERTSON, WILLIAM, in Yorkville, Wisconsin, cnf 1876 Edinburgh. [NAS.SC70.1.177/1078]

ROBERTSON, WILLIAM, in Dolton, Illinois, son of William Robertson, a mason, who died there on 27 August 1888 and his wife Mary Thomson who died 23 November 1895. [NAS.SH.7.6.1897]

ROBERTSON,....., daughter of George S. Robertson, was born in Cuba, Crawford County, Missouri, on 28 January 1872. [S#8913]

ROBERTSON,....., daughter of George S. Robertson, was born in Cuba, Crawford County, Missouri, on 13 October 1874. [S#9754]

ROBERTSON,....., son of George S. Robertson, was born in Cuba, Missouri, on 2 July 1878. [S#10,919]

ROBINSON, ISAAC, born 1808, arrived in Texas via Louisiana, settled in Refugio, Texas, died at the Battle of the Alamo on 6 March 1836. [TSHA#19.0/542][DRTL]

ROBINSON, WILLIAM, born 1826, son of John Robinson (1789-1875) and Ann Scott (1793-1865), died in Pickney, Michigan, 28 October 1870. [Lilliesleaf g/s, Roxburghshire]

ROBSON, JOHN HERON, born 1828, an advocate, son of Alexander Robson in Dumfries, died in Columbus, Texas, 21 November 1860. [AO#566][EEC#23566]

ROGER, CHARLES BROWN, born in 1854, son of Robert Roger and Agnes Brown, died in Leadville, Colorado, on 24 February 1901. [Liff g/s, Angus]; cnf Edinburgh 1901. [NAS.SC70.1.407/766]

ROMANES, ELIZABETH MARY, daughter of Robert Romanes in Craigerne, Peebles, and wife of Gilbert C. MacLagan, died in Le Mars, Iowa, on 7 March 1883. [S#12,372]

ROME, JANE HEWAT, infant daughter of Robert Moncrieff Rome jr., and Louisa Decker, died at 701 North 14th Street, St Louis, Missouri, on 14 March 1874. [AO]

ROME, STEWART MONCREIFF, third son of Thomas L. Rome a bookseller in Langholm, Dumfries-shire, died in Los Angeles on 11 December 1890. [AO: 2.1.1891]

RONALDSON, THOMAS, settled in Lorin, California, son of William Ronaldson, a farmer in Balnealhill, and his wife Margaret Stobie who died 16 November 1888. [NAS.SH.4.9.1889]

RONALDSON,......., daughter of Alexander Robertson jr., was born in the Grange, Lemars, Iowa, on 15 January 1883. [S#12,340]

ROSE, GEORGE H., a surgeon and dentist in San Francisco, California, 21 August 1855. [NAS.RS.Nairn#6/143]

ROSE, JOHN arrived in Yerba Buena, San Francisco, California, in 1840, a shipbuilder. [SHR#153]

ROSE, JOHN PRINGLE, in Uvas Valley, Gilroy, California, cnf 1889 Edinburgh. [NAS.SC70.1.272]

ROSS, JAMES, born in Scotland during 1831, died in San Francisco on 10 July 1873. [SF Daily Morning Call, 11.7.1873]

ROSS, JAMES, son of James Ross a weaver in Dunning, Perthshire, settled in Salt Lake City, Utah, before 1869. [NAS.SH.20.4.1869]

ROSS, JAMES, from Glasgow, later at East 46th Street, Chicago, cnf Edinburgh 1900. [NAS.SC70.1.386/193]

ROSS, MARY, born 1822, third daughter of James Ross a shipbuilder in Leith, and wife of David Moyes jr from Edinburgh, died in Pontoosue, Hancock County, Illinois, on 16 February 1879. [S#11,134]

ROSS, MARY ANNE, second daughter of John Ross, 79 Great King Street, Edinburgh, married Russell Robertson, HM Consul in Yokohama, in San Francisco, California, on 18 October 1883. [S#12,565]

ROSS, MICHAEL A., youngest son of Robert Ross in Dunfermline, Fife, died in Denver on 30 August 1889. [FFP]

ROSS, WILLIAM, son of Donald Ross a cooper in Invergordon, Ross and Cromarty, settled in Wilton, Waseca County, Minnesota, before 1869.[NAS.SH.18.12.1869]

ROSSIE, WILLIAM SUTHERLAND, son of John Rossie a fish curer in Orkney, settled in Illinois before 1857. [NAS.SH.14.9.1857]

ROWAND, ANDREW, a farmer in Pollo, Illinois, 1868. [NAS.SH.22.7.1868]

ROXBURGH, JOSEPH, born 1826, son of James Roxburgh, High Street, Annan, Dumfries-shire, died in Benicia, Solara, California, 20 April 1880. [AO:28.5.1880]

ROY, ANTHONY, born in 1871, son of John Roy and Janet McCreath, died in Pocatello, Idaho, on 8 January 1901. [Straiton g/s, Ayrshire]

RULE, JENNIE, daughter of Robert Rule of Westerkirk, Dumfries-shire, wife of Donald Murchison, died in Toulon, Stark County, Illinois, on 27 January 1878. [AO]

RULE, THOMAS, only son of William Rule late farmer in Violet Bank, Annan, Dumfries-shire, died in Houghton County, Lake Sysiner, Michigan, on 10 March 1866. [AO]

RUSSELL, ADAM, a joiner from Edinburgh, died at Lake Forrest, Chicago, on 8 July 1863. [S#2540]

RUSSELL, CARRIE, daughter of Reverend David Russell in Dunfermline, Fife, married James Young Beveridge from Fresno, in Vermont, California on 20 March 1890. [FH]

RUSSELL, DAVID LAURIE, in Basaltie Canyon, Gold Gulch, Yuma, Arizona, son of John Russell of Middlefield, Cupar, Fife, 1876. [NAS.SC20.34.52.268-272]

RUSSELL, ELIZABETH, born in 1822, died in San Francisco, California, on 8 August 1888. [Mertoun g/s, Berwickshire]

RUSSELL, JAMES, of the Bank of British Columbia in San Francisco, cnf Edinburgh 1898. [NAS.SC70.1.366/722]

RUSSEL, JAMES, born in 1815, son of William Russel, 'late of California', died during 1904. [Kinnedar g/s, Morayshire]

RUSSELL, JAMES, born in 1868, son of James Russell and Barbara Scott, died in San Francisco on 22 November 1897. [Cupar g/s, Fife]; cnf 1898. [NAS.SC70.1.366]

RUSSELL, JOHN, son of David Russell and Janet Campbell in Gallatown, Kirkcaldy, Fife, settled in San Francisco by 1853. [NAS.SH.19.4.1853]

RUSSELL, JOHN, born 1815, from Edinburgh, died in Kansas City on 7 January 1883. [S#12,337]

RUSSELL, WILLIAM, a miner in Kansas, cnf 1881 Edinburgh. [NAS.SC70.1.211/151]

RUTHERFORD, ARCHIBALD SCOTT, in St Louis, Missouri, cnf Edinburgh 1899. [NAS.SC70.1.386/193]

RUTHERFORD, RONALD BLAIR, born 1853, eldest son of Walter Rutherford in Mobile, Alabama, died in Missouri, Missouri, on 1 July 1871. [S#8739]

RUTHERFORD, THOMAS SCOTT, in St Louis, Missouri, cnf Edinburgh 1900. [NAS.SC70.1.387/369]

RUXTON, JOHN, in Detroit, Michigan, by 1892, son of John Ruxton, a mechanic, and Joanna Nicoll (died 12 December 1887) in Arbroath, Angus. [NAS.SH.27.10.1892]

RYRIE, ALEXANDER, born in 1865, son of James Ryrie and Charlotte Swanson, died in San Francisco on 1 December 1900. [Olrig g/s, Caithness]

SALMOND, PETER, jr, from Torbane, Bathgate, West Lothian, married Lydia Hannagir, Otter Tail County, USA, at Parker's Prairie, Minnesota, on 27 December 1878. [S#11,100]

SANDEMAN, GEORGE, in Wisconsin, 1855. [NAS.SC48.49.25.55.151]

SANDEMAN, JAMES, in Wisconsin, 1855.
[NAS.SC48.49.25.55.151]

SANDEMAN, JOHN, in Wisconsin, 1855.
[NAS.SC48.49.25.55.151]

SANDERSON, WILHELMINA, eldest daughter of William
Sanderson a merchant in Edinburgh, married Auren Garrett a
merchant in Peoria, Illinois, at George Callendar's house in
Walnut Grove, Woodford County, Illinois, on 20 February
1856. [CM#2/751]

SANDERSON, ..., son of David T. N. Sanderson, was born in Peora,
Illinois, on 27 March 1861. [S#1822]

SAWERS, GEORGE, a farmer in Missouri, cnf 1866 Edinburgh.
[NAS.SC70.1.130.407]

SCHOLLAY, HELLEN PARIS, born in 1856, daughter of David
Schollay and Jane Simpson, died in Denver, Colorado, on 17
October 1899.[Arbroath Abbey g/s, Angus]

SCHOOLER, JAMES, born in 1823, son of John Schoolar, died in
California on 11 April 1883. [Hutton g/s, Berwickshire]

SCOTT, AGNES, wife of Robert Amos in Salt Lake City, Utah,
daughter of Ann Miller or Scott in Hawick, Roxburghshire,
who died on 23 January 1897. [NAS.SH.8.1.1897]

SCOTT, CHARLES, second son of Captain Robert Scott of the
Honorable East India Company, and of Stewartfield,
Peebles, died in New Orleans on 25 August 1872. [S#9094]

SCOTT, CHARLES, born 1854, soldier in I Company, 7th Cavalry,
died at the Battle of the Little Big Horn in June 1876. [S]

SCOTT, EDMUND, died in San Francisco on 4 November 1873.
[EC#27817]

SCOTT, ERNEST KIDDER, third son of J. Lindsay Scott of
Mollance, died in Cheyenne, Wyoming Territory, on 3
November 1876. [S#10,392]

SCOTT, Mrs FRANCES M. M., born in 1841, wife of P. W. Scott late US vice consul in Tangiers, died in St Paul's, Minnesota, on 9 March 1879.[EC#29497]

SCOTT, HELEN, born in 1780, from Paisley, Renfrewshire, wife of George Caswell, died at Wing Lake, Bloomfield township, Oakland County, Michigan, on 28 August 1844. [SG#1342]

SCOTT, JAMES, a merchant skipper based in Lima, Peru, settled in Santa Barbara, California, during 1830. [SHR#153/138]

SCOTT, JAMES, born 1856, eldest son of Robert Scott in Burnetland, Peebles-shire, died in Prescott, USA, on 1 May 1882. [S#12,168]

SCOTT, JAMES, possibly from Edinburgh, in St Paul, Minnesota, by 1891. [NAS.SH.9.12.1891]

SCOTT, JEAN, born in 1833, wife of William Taylor, died in San Francisco on 7 June 1891. [Episcopal Church g/s, Montrose, Angus]

SCOTT, JOAN, born 1 June 1848, daughter of henry Scott and Elizabeth Edgely, wife of Tom Allen, died in Aurora, Illinois. [Chirnside, Berwickshire, g/s]

SCOTT, JOHN, born 1813, a farmer from Bowden, Ancrum, Roxburghshire, died in Chicago on 18 April 1872. [S#8992]

SCOTT, JOHN, born 1826, from Kelso, Roxburghshire, died in St Louis on 3 January 1873. [S#9209]

SCOTT, JOHN R., born 1853, son of David Scott and Margaret Ritchie, died in Chicago 29 August 1889. [Girvan, Ayrshire, g/s]

SCOTT, JOHN, in Duarte, Los Angeles, 1890. [NAS.RS.Culross.5.132]

SCOTT, PATRICK, born in 1817, third son of William Scott in Aberdeen, died in Detroit on 13 September 1849. [AJ#5309]

SCOTT, PATRICK, settled at Fort Scott, Kansas, by 1889. [NAS.SH.18.9.1889]

SCOTT, ROBERT, probably from Jedburgh, Roxburghshire, a
saddler in Scotland, Oakland, California, by 1868.
[NAS.SH.10.1.1868]

SCOTT, WILLIAM, from Glasgow, then in Chicago, married
Maggie Jack, eldest daughter of John Jack in Edinburgh, at
Taylor's Hotel, Jersey City, on 12 October 1873. [S#9442]

SCOTT, ..., daughter of William C. Scott, was born at 136 Walnut
Street, Chicago, on 5 November 1874. [S#9778]

SCOTT,....., son of W.C. Scott, was born at 696 Westlake Street,
Chicago, on 9 February 1879. [S#11,109]

SCOUGAL, Dr Colonel WILLIAM S., a banker in Yankton,
Dakota, youngest son of James Scougal, HM Inspector of
Schools in Scotland, married Jessie Darling Wilson, fourth
daughter of John Wilson, a bleacher in Dunfermline, in New
York on 16 October 1884. [S#12877]

SELLER, PATRICK, from Selkirk, a manufacturer in Colorado, cnf
1891.[NAS.SC70.1.301]

SELLICK, FRANCIS WILLIAM, son of James Sellick an excise
supervisor in Burntisland, Fife, settled in Paw Paw,
Michigan, by 1877. [NAS.SH.7.3.1877]

SHAND, GEORGE, born in Huntly, Aberdeenshire, died in New
Orleans on 2 September 1839. [AJ.29.1.1840]

SHANKS, JOHN, born in 1832, a compositor, son of Colin Shanks a
baker in Aberdeen, died in Delhi, Illinois, on 19 July
1858.[AJ: 25.8.1858]

SHARON, CLARA A., wife of Francis G. Newlands, died in San
Francisco on 17 February 1882. [S#12,072]

SHARP, JAMES, born 1790 in Dundee, son of William Sharp and
Isabella Kinnear, died in New Orleans on 13 August 1829.
[Howff g/s, Dundee]

SHAW, DAVID, a farmer in Strone of Cully, Blairgowrie,
Perthshire, then in Colorado, 1871. [NAS.RS.Forfar.26.253]

SHAW, ..., son of Reverend D.E.Shaw, was born in Keokuk, Iowa, on 29 March 1882. [S#12,079]

SHEARER, J. S., from Aberdeenshire, emigrated to Poweshiek, Iowa, in 1872.[ENES#1.253]

SHEPHERD, DAVID, son of William Shepherd (1792-1832), settled in New Orleans before 1847. [Dunfermline g/s, Fife]

SHEPHERD, ELIZABETH, youngest daughter of John Shepherd from Halbeath, Fife, died in Salt Lake City, Utah, on 19 July 1873. [DJ]

SHEPHERD, JOHN MUNRO, born in 1853, son of George Shepherd andIsabel Middleton, died in Missuala, Montana, on 18 September 1902. [Rosehill g/s, Montrose, Angus]

SHERIFF, ELIZA BRAND, younger daughter of George Dick Sheriff from Kingseat, Fife, died in Walsenburg, Huerfane County, Colorado, on 10 April 1891. [DJ]

SHERWOOD, WILLIAM, possibly from Dunipace, Stirlingshire, settled in Graniteville, Nevada, before 1878. [NAS.SH.7.1.1868]

SHIELS, FRANCIS ALEXANDER, son of James Shiels from Earlston, Berwickshire, was born at Shawnee Plantation, Fannin County, Texas, on 8 October 1878. [S#10,007]

SHIELS, GEORGE DUNSMURE, born 1874, third son of George Shiles from Balgove, St Andrews, Fife, died in Oaklaw Grange, Purdy, Barry County, Missouri, on 18 October 1882. [S#12,268]

SHIELLS, or CLEMENT, JACOBINA CATHERINE, in Milwaukee by 1899. [NAS.SH.19.10.1899]

SHILLINGLAW, WILLIAM, born 1854, youngest son of James Shillinglaw in Stow, Peeblesshire, drowned in Basque River, Texas, on 16 May 1880. [S#11,510]

SHINE, TIMOTHY KIDWELL, in Texas, cnf Edinburgh 1901. [NAS.SC70.1.406/617]

SHOOLBRED, JOHN S., from Dunfermline, Fife, married Katie F. Todd in St Louis on 12 June 1884. [DJ]

SIBBALD, JOHN, late of Eilden Mains, Melrose, then of Mont Tom, California, married Luela Myers, daughter of Mr Samuels, at Sonoma, California, in November 1874. [S#9811]

SIBBALD, MARY W., born in 1825, daughter of David Sibbald and Anne Sibbald, died in California on 8 November 1853. [St Peter's g/s, Dundee]

SIM, GEORGE C., born in 1850, son of William Sim [1821-1893] and Mary Stewart [1824-1908] in Braemar, settled in California by 1878, died in San Francisco during 1906. [Braemar g/s, Aberdeenshire] [NAS.GD1.756.2]

SIMSON, ..., daughter of Thomas and Agnes Simson, born 1 August 1881, died at 373 West 14th Street, Chicago, on 14 August 1881. [S#11,902]

SIMPSON, ALEXANDER, born in Dingwall during 1811, a Hudson Bay Company trader temporarily in Monterey and in San Francisco around 1840. [DCB#7/808]

SIMPSON, Mrs BATHIA SOUTER, daughter of Thomas Wright in Banff, and wife of Alexander Simpson from Macduff, Banffshire, died in Illinois on 20 September 1860. [AJ: 24.10.1860]

SIMPSON, CHARLES NAPIER, in Kansas City, Missouri, son of the late William Simpson, a farmer in Bishopton, Whithorn, and his wife Elizabeth McKenna who died 27 July 1891. [NAS.SH.10.9.1897]

SIMPSON, WILLIAM KINNEAR, son of David Simpson in Dundee, settled in Silver City, Utah, by 1873. [NAS.SH.20.8.1873]

SIMPSON, WILLIAM, a storekeeper in Chicago by 1880. [NAS.SH.23.8.1880]

SINCLAIR, CATHERINE, born 1810, daughter of Donald Sinclair (1781-1867) and Catherine Thompson (1788-1865), wife of George Robin, died in Wisconsin during 1851.

SINCLAIR, HENRY WILLIAM, married Margaret Emily Wollaston, in Fairmont, Minnesota, on 24 October 1878. [EC#29377]

SINCLAIR, JOHN, a trapper and newspaper editor, arrived in California in 1840, agent for John Sutter, granted El Paso Rancho north of New Helvetia.[SHR#153/142]

SINCLAIR, JOHN SUTHERLAND, born 1858, emigrated to America 1875, farmer in North Dakota, Earl of Caithness 1891. [Scots Peerage #II.359]

SINCLAIR, Mrs MARGARET, born in Islay, Argyll, wife of Duncan Sinclair, died in New Orleans on 14 February 1878. [S#10,852]

SINCLAIR, PETER, from Waterloo Place, Edinburgh, died in Chicago on 25 February 1869. [S#7995]

SINCLAIR, VIRGINIA GEORGINA MALCOLM, youngest daughter of John Sinclair, married Ferdinand Vassault in San Francisco on 26 September 1853. [EEC#22515]

SKENE, CHARLOTTE, born in 1847, eldest daughter of William Skene, formerly of Banchory Ternan, Aberdeenshire, wife of J. C. Rawlins, died in Pleasant Valley, Jo Davis County, Illinois, on 14 February 1876. [AJ#6689]

SKINNER, WILLIAM, second son of John Skinner, died in St Louis on 23 August 1869. [S#8152]

SLOANE, ANTHONY, born 1794, son of Anthony Sloane and Jane Lowrie, settled in New Orleans, died in Whithorn, Kirkcudbrightshire, on 13 December 1835. [NAS.SH]

SLOAN, ELIZABETH, in Salt Lake City, cnf 1888 Edinburgh. [NAS.SC70.1.265]

SLOANE, PETER, from Kirkcudbright, died in New Orleans on 18 May 1829. [NAS.SH]

SLOSS, DUNCAN, son of Andrew Sloss [1782-1847], died in California aged 45. [Colmonell g/s, Ayrshire]

SMALL, EDWARD PATRICK, settled in Lakeville, California, son of Joseph Small, a pawnbroker in Hamilton, Lanarkshire, who died 11 February 1888.[NAS.SH.26.7.1889]

SMART, ANNE CHRISTIAN, daughter of James Smart and granddaughter of James Gray a writer in Cupar, Fife, died in Kansas City on 21 July 1877. [S#10,626]

SMART, CHARLES MORTON, born 1845, youngest son of Reverend Dr Smart in Leith, died in Chicago on 29 August 1882. [S#12,222]

SMART, DAVID, possibly from Kirkcaldy, Fife, settled in Michigan by 1852. [NAS.SH.8.4.1852]

SMART, JAMES KYD, in Chicago by 1896, grandson of George Ramsay in Arbroath, Angus, who died on 19 September 1864, and son of Alexander Smart, a manufacturer, Hill Place, Arbroath, and his wife Mary Ramsay who died 13 August 1896. [NAS.SH.5.11.1896]

SMART, JOHN, born 1797, a laborer, emigrated via Port Glasgow on the Elizabeth, master A. Grierson, bound for New Orleans to settle in Louisiana, arrived in New Orleans 12 November 1827. [USNA.M259/7]

SMART, ROBERT, a seaman from St Monance, Fife, died in San Francisco in October 1849. [PR.26.1.1850]

SMITH, AGNES M., third daughter of John W. Smith from Loanhead, Midlothian, married John K. Mitchell, in Detroit, Michigan, on 27 June 1883. [S#12,485]

SMITH, ALEXANDER BURT, born 1844, son of William Smith a printer in Edinburgh, died in Reno, Nevada, on 5 October 1872. [S#9133]

SMITH, Mrs ANN, born in Edinburgh during 1822, died in San Francisco on 27 December 1898. [SF Daily Morning Call, 29.12.1898]

SMITH, ARTHUR EVERARD, in Omaha, Nebraska, cnf 1893 Edinburgh. [NAS.SC70.1.323]

SMITH, AVARD, born in Scotland during 1842, died at sea on 3 October 1885.[Daily Alta California, 8.12.1885]

SMITH, DAVID, late a merchant in the Bahamas, died on his plantation in Louisiana on 24 April 1813. [EA#5218/423]

SMITH, DAVID, died in Attacapas, Louisiana, on 14 February 1829. [EEC#18318]

SMITH, GEORGE, Baxter Springs, Cherokee, Kansas, 1891. [NAS.RS.Kintore.5.283]

SMITH, ELIZABETH ANN, eldest daughter of Robert Smith a brassfounder in Viewforth Cottage, Kirkcaldy, Fife, married Arthur Gun, in Galveston, Texas, on 13 September 1874. [S#9736]

SMITH or STEPHEN, ELISABETH, Roundtop Farm, Harrisville, Randolph County, Indiana, 1891. [NAS.RS.Kintore.5.283]

SMITH, ESTHER, born in 1853, wife of Robert Russell a builder in Denver, Colorado, died in Dunfermline, Fife, during 1891. [FH,4.3.1891]

SMITH, GEORGE, from Old Deer, Aberdeenshire, emigrated to America in 1833, a land speculator in Illinois, banker in Chicago in 1839, President of the Chicago, Milwaukee and St Paul Railroad. [ENES#1.253]

SMITH, GEORGE, at Baxter Springs, Cherokee, Kansas, 19 September 1891. [NAS.RS.Kintore#5/283]

SMITH, HELEN, youngest daughter of Matthew Smith, Easter Bush, Edinburgh, married Charles Lonie, a joiner from Edinburgh, in Kansas City on 30 November 1870. [S#8556]

SMITH, HERBERT BOULGER, infant son of George Smith and Catherine Hall Smith, died at Gardener House, Chicago, on 25 May 1879. [S#11,200]

SMITH, JAMES, born 15 September 1800, a tailor in Bordland, Kansas, died on 9 January 1869. [Newlands g/s, Peebles-shire]

SMITH, JAMES, jr., from Edinburgh then in Cincinatti, Ohio, married Lizzie Porter, youngest daughter of William Porter, Kilree, Jerrit's Pass, Ireland, in Indianapolis, Indiana, on 7 August 1882. [S#12,205]

SMITH, JAMES H., Harrisville Mills, Randolph County, Indiana, 1891. [NAS.RS.Kintore.5.283]

SMITH, JOHN, jr, from Loanhead, Midlothian, married Elizabeth Hinchcliffe Cowls from London, at 525 Congress East, Detroit, on 26 November 1872. [S#9171]

SMITH, JOHN, a hardware merchant in New Orleans in 1878. [NAS.RS.Forfar#34/132]

SMITH, JOHN, Union City, Indiana, 1891. [NAS.RS.Kintore.5.283]

SMITH, JOHN ALLAN, sometime of Travers City, Michigan, then in Cook County, Illinois, died in Jefferson City, cnf Edinburgh 1901. [NAS.SC70.1.400/748]

SMITH, MARIA, born in 1843, daughter of Alexander Smith and Barbara Guthrie, died in San Francisco on 12 September 1882. [Arbroath g/s, Angus]

SMITH, MICHAEL, born in Stirling, son of Hugh Smith and Mary Robertson, married Maria Antonia Rillieux from New Orleans, in Louisiana on 13 April 1801. [LGS]

SMITH, WILLIAM EBENEZER, probably from Edinburgh, an engineer in Aurora, Illinois, by 1868. [NAS.SH.17.11.1868]

SMITH, WILLIAM GRIERSON, from Edinburgh, married Emma Gray Ryder, daughter of Captain Redmond S. Ryder, in Detroit, Michigan, on 1 August 1876. [S#10,318]

SMITH, WILLIAM R., Union City, Indiana, 1891. [NAS.RS.Kintore.5.283]

SMITH, WILLIAM T., a miller, third son of William Smith, manager of the Stockbridge Mills, Edinburgh, married Elizabeth Fair Mitchell, eldest daughter of William Mitchell, from Dundee, a mill proprietor in Detroit, Michigan, there on 30 December 1875. [S#10,152]

SMITH, ..., son of Robert Smith from Glasgow, was born in St Paul, Minnesota, on 14 November 1871. [S#8846]

SMITH,......, son of Andrew Smith from Edinburgh, was born in Detroit on 13 April 1877. [S#10,539]

SMITH,......, daughter of William Grierson Smith from Edinburgh, was born in Detroit on 20 May 1877. [S#10,570]

SMITH, ..., son of Andrew Smith was born in Detroit, Michigan, on 19 May 1879. [S#11,194]

SMITH, ..., son of Andrew Smith, was born in Detroit on 21 October 1881. [S#11,954]

SOMERVILLE, MARY, relict of Reverend William Home, Braehead, Lanarkshire, died in Yorktown, Delaware County, Indiana, on 15 April 1850. [W#1110]

SOMERVILLE, MARY, younger daughter of James Somerville a solicitor in Edinburgh, married William Fisher a merchant in New Westminster, British Columbia, in San Francisco on 29 August 1871. [S#8785]

SOMERVILLE, WILLIAM, born 1788, third son of John Somerville [1754-1811] and Janet Somerville [1753-1803], died at Clear Creek, Monoie County, Indiana, 7 September 1821. [St Andrew's g/s, Peebles]

SOMERVILLE, ..., daughter of Thomas Somerville a blacksmith, was born in Keokuk, Iowa, on 7 February 1873. [AO]

SOUTTER, WILLIAM, probably from Angus, died in California on 21 November 1863. [NAS.SH.7.10.1856; 2.4.1873]

SOUTHWARD, JOHN SCOTT, only son of M. Southward, and grandson of Simon Scott of Carlyle Place, Annan, Dumfriesshire, died in St Paul, Minnesota, on 1 June 1873. [AO]

SPALDING, ALEXANDER S., an engineer, married Euphemia T. Ross, eldest daughter of David Ross, Langness Lighthouse, Isle of Man, in Clinton, Iowa, on 3 May 1882. [S#12,108]

SPENCE, DAVID, arrived in California in 1824, a merchant in Monterey, Member of the Legislative Council, died after 1857. [SHR#153/138]

SPENCER, AMBROSE HALL, in Los Angeles, cnf 1896 Edinburgh. [NAS.SC70.1.350]

SPIERS, JAMES, son of James Spiers in Neilston, Renfrewshire, settled as an engineer in San Francisco by 1882. [NAS.SH.18.5.1882]

SPOWART, MARGARET, born in 1826, wife of John Banks from Dunfermline, Fife, died in Franklin, Idaho, Utah, on 6 August 1888. [DJ]

SPROAT, ROBERT, born in 1837, son of Hugh Sproat and Mary MacMillan, died in Emmith, Idaho, on 26 March 1925. [Senwick g/s]

SPROUL, HUGH, born in Scotland during 1818, died in San Francisco on 21 November 1865. [SF Daily Examiner, 22.11.1865]

SQUAIR, JAMES, President of the 1st National Bank, Cedar Rapids, Boone County, Nebraska, 1908. [NAS.RS.Nairn.34.61]

STACPOOLE, RICHARD C., born 1849, eldest son of G. C. Stacpoole, MD, died in San Antonio, Texas, on 21 May 1877. [EC#28923]

STARK, ADAM BERTRAM, son of James Stark of Huntsfield, Lanarkshire, married Eveline Hightree, eldest daughter of Dr Hightree of Civilbend, Missouri, there on 12 March 1871, [S#8641]; he died at Civilbend, Missouri, on 28 February 1877. [EC#28858]

STARK, JAMES, nephew of James Ferguson a manufacturer in Aberdeen, and for many years his agent in Halifax, Nova Scotia, died in Oregon Territory, in June 1843. [AJ#5012]

STARK, JAMES, son of James Stark of Huntfield, Ayrshire, died in Civilbend, Missouri, on 27 February 1877. [S#10,508]

STEEL, GEORGE, born in Biggar, Lanarkshire, 1798, a clothier
from Edinburgh, died in Rock Island, Illinois, on 14
November 1873. [S#9481]

STEELE, JOHN, youngest son of James Steele, 58 Nicolson Street,
Edinburgh, was killed by Mexican Indians near San Diego,
Texas, on 17 April 1878. [S#10,889]

STEEL, or FREEMAN, LILIAS, in Genesee, Waukesha County,
Wisconsin, 1870. [NAS.SC48.49.25]

STEEL, THOMAS, MD, in Genesee, Waukesha County, Wisconsin,
1870. [NAS.SC49.48.25.70/86]

STEEPLES, ELLEN ISABELLA, born 1875, daughter of Francis
and Mary Steeples, died in Des Moines, Iowa, on 2
December 1876. [S#10,439]

STEEPLES, FRANCIS O., son of William Steeples a painter in
Musselburgh, Midlothian, died in Qurich, Brooks County,
Kansas, on 29 April 1881. [S#11,809]

STEEPLES, ..., son of Francis Steeples, was born at Blue Island
Avenue, Chicago, on 16 February 1873. [S#9238]

STEEPLES, ..., daughter of Francis Steeples, was born at 191
Forquier Street, Chicago, on 27 December 1874. [S#9829]

STEPHEN, ALEXANDER, Roundtop Farm, Harrisville, Randolph
County, Indiana, 1891. [NAS.RS.Kintore.5.283]

STEPHEN, JOHN, born in 1840, son of James Stephen and Jane
Craig, died in Alameda, California, on 13 July 1892.
[Dunnottar g/s, Kincardineshire]

STEPHENS, JOHN GEORGE, in Prospect, Los Angeles,
California, cnf 1898 Edinburgh. [NAS.SC70.1.371/378]

STEPHEN, ROBERT, jr., born in 1810, late a farmer in Balbride,
Durris, Kincardineshire, died in Knoxville, Knox County,
Illinois, on 4 March 1844. [AJ#6024]

STEPHENS, WILLIAM W., Spring Valley, youngest son of J.
Stephens formerly in Montrose, Angus, married Elizabeth
Peddie, only daughter of John Peddie in Montrose, at the

International Hotel, Toano, Nevada, on 16 December 1873.
[S#9503]

STEPHEN, WILLIAM, born 1852, son of William Stephen in West
Cults, Aberdeenshire, died in San Diego, Texas, on 26
October 1878. [AJ.4.11.1878]

STEVEN, J., arrived in San Francisco from Glasgow on board the
barque <u>Madeira</u>, Captain Douglas, on 9 November 1851.
[SFL#3/2]

STEVEN, JEANNIE, daughter of Williamson Steven a hairdresser
in Edinburgh, relict of James Morrison and wife of Jeremiah
Gaffney, died in San Francisco on 26 November 1870.
[S#8573]

STEVEN, THOMAS SOMERVILLE, fourth son of William
Steven, West Register Street, Edinburgh, died in Sacramento
City, California, in 1860. [S#1730]

STEVENSON, AGNES, from Edinburgh, settled in San Francisco,
cnf 1891 Edinburgh. [NAS.SC70.1.258]

STEVENSON, ANDREW J., born in Melrose 1814, second son of
Andrew Stevenson a forester in Longnewton,
Roxburghshire, died in San Jose, California, 1875. [S#9996]

STEVENSON, ANDREW MCMATH, in San Francisco, cnf 1891
Edinburgh. [NAS.SC70.1.299]

STEVENSON, DAVID, born in 1876, son of James Stevenson and
Jane Blair, died in Thermopolis, Wyoming, on 18 September
1909.[Kirkoswald g/s, Ayrshire]

STEVENSON, ROBERT, possibly from Neilston, Renfrewshire,
settled as a joiner in Sparta, Randulf County, Illinois, by
1868. [NAS.SH.22.5.1868]

STEVENSON, ROBERT LOUIS, from Edinburgh, married Fanny
Van De Grift Osbourne from Indiana, in San Francisco on 19
May 1880. [S#11,519]

STEVENSON, WILLIAM, born in 1826, son of Robert Stevenson
[1796-1875], and Marion Watson [1797-1826], died in
Illinois on 26 June 1905.[Fenwick g/s, Ayrshire]

STEWART, ALEXANDER ALLAN, born 1832, son of Alexander Stewart (1778-1831), a manufacturer in Bridgeton, and his wife Margaret Allan (1799-1838), died in Chicago on 9 April 1864. [Bridgeton g/s, Glasgow]

STEWART, ALEXANDER, born in 1818, son of Walter Stewart and Mary Hill, died at Colorado Springs on 17 April 1884. [Forfar g/s, Angus]

STEWART, ANDREW DAVID, born 3 September 1813, son of James A. Stewartand his wife Charlotte Stewart, died in Missouri 17 April 1848. [Moulin g/s, Perthshire]

STEWART, CHRISTOPHER, born 1780, emigrated to USA in 1804, a planter in New Orleans. [1812]

STEWART, EDWARD GEORGE, youngest son of William Stewart of Shambellie, died in Marshall, Salino, Missouri, on 31 December 1876. [EC#28788]; cnf 1878. [NAS.SC70.1.187/155]

STEWART, EDWARD GEORGE, in Saline County, Missouri, died 31 December 1876, possibly from New Abbey, Kirkcudbrightshire. [NAS.SH.8.7.1899]

STEWART, or GILSTRAP, ELLEN JANE, in Racine, Missouri, 1887, daughter of Thomas Stewart in Fall Clove, New York, who died 14 October 1855, and niece of Elizabeth Stewart, in Castlepark, Auchterarder, Perthshire, who died 23 April 1880. [NAS.SH.1887]

STEWART, FRANK BEATTIE, in Fletcher, Oregon, 1888, brother of David Stewart an advocate in Aberdeen who died 8 February 1888.[NAS.SH.2.7.1888]

STEWART, HENRY, from Aberdeen, a sailor on the <u>Jupiter of New York</u>, died in California 1823. [AJ#4036]

STEWART, Mrs JANE, born in Scotland, wife of John Stewart, died in San Francisco during July 1875. [San Francisco Daily Morning Call, 9.7.1875]

STEWART, JOHN, a Lieutenant of the Carolina Highlanders Regiment, died in Woodville, New Orleans, brother of Alexander A. Stewart, Administration, October 1827, PCC

STEWART, KATE, daughter of Fergus Stewart and Mary Graham Sinclair, died in Denver on 14 November 1886. [Kilnonver g/s, Argyll]

STEWART, MUNGO, son of Duncan Stewart in Pitlochry, Perthshire, died at his brother's house in Zavala, Texas, on 28 August 1876. [AJ#6715][S#10,344]

STEWART, WILLIAM, possibly from Dalmellington, Ayrshire, settled in Exeter, Michigan, by 1877. [NAS.SH.24.12.1877]

STEWART, Sir WILLIAM DRUMMOND, [1795-1871], soldier, adventurer and explorer of the West. [NAS.GD121]

STIRLING, ALEXANDER, a planter near St Francisville, Louisiana. [1812]

STIRLING, Mr ANNIE, wife of Mathew R. Stirling, died in San Francisco on 1 December 1873. [SF Daily Morning Call, 3.12.1873]

STIRLING, JOHN HARTLEY, born 1861, second son of John Stirling of Fairburn, Ross-shire, died in San Francisco on 22 October 1884. [S#12884]

STIRLING, WILLIAM R., third son of John Stirling of Kippendavie, married Alice Hibbard, daughter of William G. Hibbard, in Gracechurch, Chicago, on 26 April 1883. [S#12,415]

STIRLING, ..., daughter of W. R. Stirling, was born in Chicago on 12 March 1884. [EC#31039][S#12,692]

STIVEN, WILLIAM, of the firm Stiven and MacLeod, Chartered Accountants in Glasgow, drowned in the Calumet River near Pullman, Illinois, on 29 June 1884. [S#12805]

STOCKS, DAVID, eldest son of Alexander Stocks late of Dalkeith, Midlothian, died in Santa Barbara on 18 June 1882. [S#12,181]

STODDART, ALEXANDER, youngest son of Captain Robert Stoddart in Bo'ness, West Lothian, died in Ypsilanti, Michigan, in 1874. [S#9786]

STODART, ARCHIBALD, born in 1846, son of Archibald Stodart and Agnes Robertson, died in Buena Park, California, on 24 December 1913.[Covington g/s, Lanarkshire]

STODDART, JOHN, husband of Ann Reid, father of John, settled in Fond du Lac, Wisconsin, before 1852. [NAS.SH.9.2.1865]

STODDARD, ROBERT, born in Scotland during 1830, died in San Francisco during October 1863. [SF Daily Alta California, 16.10.1863]

STOTT, ELIZABETH, born in 1853, wife of F. Gaynor, died in San Francisco on 1 December 1889. [St Cuthbert's g/s, Edinburgh]

STRACHAN, ALEXANDER, from Blairgowrie, Perthshire, a farmer in Cook County, Illinois, 1872. [NAS.SC49.48.25.71/184]

STRACHAN, WILLIAM, in St Louis, Missouri, 1851. [NAS.SC49.48.25.51/217]

STRATH, JOHN, born in 1839, son of William Strath, in Glack of Botriphnie, Banffshire, died in Chicago on 25 May 1870. [AJ:15.6.1870]

STRATHEARN, JAMES, settled in Lassa, Illinois, before 1877. [NAS.SH.4.6.1877]

STRONACH, ISABELLA, relict of James Watkins a merchant in Aberdeen, died at 470 15th Street, Detroit, on 21 March 1876. [AJ#6691]

STUART, DAVID KNOX, a physician in New Orleans, son of John Stuart of East Kilbride, Lanarkshire, died in New Orleans on 10 April 1851, cnf 1853 Edinburgh. [W#1248][NAS.SC70.1.81]

SUMNER, AGNES, relict of Thomas Sumner in Edinburgh, died at the residence of her son-in-law in Chicago on 15 January 1880. [S#11,407]

SUMNER, FRANCIS, son of Francis Sumner in Kelso, Roxburghshire, died at Douglas Station, Monterey County, California, in June 1874, buried in Salinas, California. [S#9689]

SUTHERLAND, ALEXANDER SMITH, formerly in New Orleans, late in New York, Administration, October 1828, PCC

SUTHERLAND, CHRISTINA, born in 1857, daughter of James Sutherland and Margaret Cumming, wife of James Sutherland, died on 17 March 1893, buried in Denver. [Ballachy g/s]

SUTHERLAND, GEORGE SINCLAIR, died in Fond du Lac, Wisconsin, during August 1870. [NAS.GD139/509]

SUTHERLAND, WILLIAM SMITH, in California, cnf 1867 Edinburgh. [NAS.SC70.1.137]

SWAN, CATHERINE, eldest daughter of William Swan, Queen Anne Street, Dunfermline, Fife, married William Gilchrist from Tecumseh, Michigan, in Dunfermline on 3 February 1846. [EEC#21304]

SWAN, WILLIAM TAYLOR, born 1866, youngest son of James Swan, High Street, Hawick, died at 34 Adams Avenue, Detroit, on 27 July 1884. [S#12,824]

SWAN, JOHN, born in 1870, died in San Francisco on 10 May 1887.[Dalbeattie g/s, Kirkcudbrightshire]

SWANSON, JOHN GOODFELLOW, son of Donald Swanson and Janet Goodfellow in Langside, Peebles, a rigger in San Francisco by 1867.[NAS.SH.16.11.1867]

SWANSTON, CHRISTINA, youngest daughter of James Swanston, Edinburgh, married Henry Myers from Indiana, at Salano Street, corner of Mississippi Street, Potrero, San Francisco, on 10 November 1875. [S#10098]

SWANSTON, MARY, daughter of James Swanston, Marshall Meadows, Berwick-on-Tweed, wife of Alexander Guthrie,

died in San Rafael.California, on 25 June 1874.
[EC#28002][S#9654]

SYME, ANDREW, in New Orleans, brother of Hugh Syme.
Administration, January 1821 PCC

SYME, JANET, born in 1842, fourth daughter of Henry and
Margaret Syme in Bridge Street, Dunfermline, Fife, wife of
J. G. Bain, died at Council Bluffs, Iowa, during 1870. [DP:
2.4.1870] [S#8319]

TAIT, MAGGIE C., eldest daughter of James Tait a shepherd in
Balado, Kinross, married John F. Johnson, at Waltham, La
Salle County, Illinois, on 17 February 1875. [S#9876]

TAIT, MARGARET, daughter of John Tait in Minnigaff,
Kirkcudbrightshire, wife of .... Gibson, settled in Rockford,
Illinois, by 1838. [NAS.SH.3.2.1838]

TARBAT, ALEXANDER, a plasterer from Forfar, son of Marjery
Rose or Tarbat in Forfar, Angus, settled in California by
1857. [NAS.SH.30.9.1857][NAS.RS.Forfar.18.206]

TATE, JOHN, from the Orkney Islands, settled at Fort Vancouver,
Oregon, probate January 1855 PCC

TAYLOR, ANDREW, from Caithness, married Elizabeth, daughter
of Findlay Mackay in Caithness, in Rampart Street, New
Orleans, on 11 March 1874. [S#9581]

TAYLOR, DAVID, a solicitor's clerk in San Francisco, 1865.
[NAS.SC49.48.25.66/134, 189]

TAYLOR, GEORGE, born in 1802, late of the Mill of Inchmarlo,
Upper Banchory, Aberdeenshire, died in Detroit, Michigan,
on 9 July 1849. [AJ#5303]

TAYLOR, GEORGE, eldest son of Peter Taylor, was killed by
Indians near Wickenburg, Arizona, on 11 March 1873.
[S#9373]

TAYLOR, HUGH, son of Donald Taylor, died in Nevada during
October 1890. [Dornoch g/s, Sutherland]

TAYLOR, JAMES BANKS, fourth son of Alexander Taylor in
West Seaton Mains, Prestonpans, East Lothian, died in New
York on his way home from California on 31 January 1884.
[EC#31004]

TAYLOR, JOHN, born in 1841, brother of W. L. Taylor, a
bookseller in Peterhead, Aberdeenshire, died in Nashville,
Tennessee, on 24 November 1863 of wounds received at the
Battle of Chickamanga, on 20 September 1863 in which he
served as a Sergeant of the 96th Illinois Volunteers. [AJ:
30.12.1863] [S#2660]

TAYLOR, WILLIAM, a farmer from Thomastown, Drumblade,
Aberdeenshire, died on passage from New Orleans to St
Louis on 30 March 1842. [AJ: 8.6.1842]

TEASDALE, HUGH, from Larkhall, Lanarkshire, settled in Dallas,
Illinois, by 1851. [NAS.RH1.2.764]

TELFER, ISABELLA, born in 1834, wife of Andrew Davidson and
grand -daughter of William Telfer in Linlithgow, West
Lothian, died in Chicago on 17 March 1873. [EC#27613]

TELFER, JOHN, born 1810, from Grove Street, Musselburgh, died
in Morris, Grundy County, Illinois, on 9 April 1874.
[S#9600]

TEMPLETON, THOMAS, from Glasgow, died in Chicago on 30
November 1881, cnf 5 May 1882 Edinburgh.
[NAS.SC70.1.214/550] [His wife Mary Galbraith and their
children Thomas and Mary also in Chicago.]

TENNANT, ROBERT GRAY, a produce dealer in Chicago by
1890, son of William Gray Tennant a merchant in Leith and
Janet Walker who died 1 August 1872.
[NAS.SH.26.11.1890]

THIN, ROBERT, in Chicago, 1887, son of Robert Thin and Isabella
Clouston who died 18 November 1884. [NAS.SH.5.8.1887]

THIRD, ELSPET, from Aberdeenshire, widow of Lewis Burnett,
died in Lockport, Illinois, on 13 April 1858. [AJ: 16.6.1858]

THOM, WILLIAM, son of William Thom a farmer in Glasgoforest, Kinnellar, Aberdeenshire, died in St Charles, Illinois, on 25 January 1852.[AJ : 10.3.1852]

THOMSON, ALEXANDER, born in 1796, from Fife, died in West Port, Wisconsin, on 17 April 1876. [EC#28584]

THOMSON, ANDREW L., born 1822, brother of the late William L. Thomson in Toothills, Annan, Dumfries-shire, died at Honey Creek, Marengo, Iowa, on 8 January 1899. [AO: 3.2.1899]

THOMSON, CATHERINE, born 1864, daughter of John Thomson, grand-daughter of William Thomson in Gretna, Dumfries-shire, died at Poncha Springs, Colorado, on 12 June 1887. [AO:8.7.1887]

THOMSON, COLIN, settled in Duluth before 1889. [NAS.SH.25.7.1889]

THOMSON, EMILY IDA, in Michigan, cnf 1882 Edinburgh. [NAS.SC70.1.218]

THOMSON, FRANCIS, late of Charlesfield Bar, died in Washington, Fillimore County, Minnesota, 7 September 1893. [AO:16.10.1893]

THOMSON, GEORGE, probably from Galashiels, Selkirkshire, settled in St Louis before 1869. [NAS.SH.18.1.1869]

THOMSON, GEORGE, in Chicago by 1896, son of Duncan MacLaren Thomson, probably from Stirling, a real estate agent in Chicago who died there on 7 January 1896. [NAS.SH.25.9.1896]

THOMSON, HUGH MAIR, born 1812, son of Isaac Thomson in Toothills, Annan, Dumfries-shire, settled at Ellerlie farm, Davenport, Winfield township, Scott County, Iowa, in 1844, died 1887. [AO.25.3.1887]

THOMSON, JAMES, probably from Aberdeen, settled in Chicago by 1882. [NAS.SH.14.10.1882]

THOMSON, JAMES, in Emporia, Kansas, cnf 1884 Edinburgh. [NAS.SC70.1.231/15]

THOMSON, JAMES, in Denver, Colorado, 1887, son of James
Thomson in Aberdeen who died 23 November 1886.
[NAS.SH.28.3.1887]

THOMSON, JAMES, in Jacksonville, Oregon, son of William
Thomson a slater and shipowner in Stonehaven,
Kincardineshire, who died 28 January 1849.
[NAS.SH.9.5.1888]

THOMSON, JAMES, from Earlston, Berwickshire, died at Point
Huron, Michigan, on 2 July 1874. [S#9672]

THOMSON, JANET, wife of William Brown a cattle dealer from
Edinburgh, died in Chicago on 23 June 1881. [S#11,860]

THOMSON, JEAN, in Rosenden, Cairo, Illinois, cnf 1853
Edinburgh. [NAS.SC70.1.79]

THOMSON, JESSIE, in Chicago, cnf 1893 Edinburgh.
[NAS.SC70.1.321]

THOMPSON, JOHN, coal miner, settled in Belleville, Nebraska,
1857, Nebraska City 1859, Alton, Illinois, 1859-1860, joined
US Army 1861-1864, returned to Alton, Illinois, married
Betsey Haig in 1865, settled in West Belleville, St Clair
County, Illinois, by 1872, in Kansas 1881. [StAUL:MS#32]

THOMSON, JOHN, eldest son of George Thomson a carriage
builder in Stirling, died in Makeira, Illinois, on 22 November
1883. [S#12,606]

THOMSON, JOHN, in Frankfort Station, Will County, Illinois, cnf
1884 Edinburgh. [NAS.SC70.1.237/298]

THOMSON, MARY, in Chicago, cnf 1896 Edinburgh.
[NAS.SC70.1.315]

THOMPSON, PETER, MH, born 1854, from Markinch, Fife,
soldier of the 7th Cavalry in 1876. [S]

THOMSON, PETER, born in 1824, son of Peter Thomson and
Catherine Thomson, a merchant in San Francisco, died in
Oakland, California, on 9 August 1901. [Milnathort g/s,
Kinross-shire]

THOMSON, THOMAS, a merchant in Louisiana, married Isabella
Tweedie, third daughter of Alexander Tweedie a merchant in
Edinburgh, at Gayfield Square, Edinburgh, on 20 October
1824. [BM#16/614]

THOMSON, THOMAS GRAY, a chemist and druggist, youngest
son of Thomas Thomson, Buccleuch Place, Dalkeith,
Midlothian, died in Grand Rapids, on 24 July 1869.
[S#8125]

THOMSON, WILLIAM, born in Edinburgh during 1777, a
silversmith in New York, died in Clinton, Michigan, on 18
October 1833. [ANY.2.74]

THOMSON, WILLIAM, son of James Thomson a tailor in
Arbroath, Angus, settled in Clinton, Iowa, before 1872.
[NAS.SH.24.6.1872]

THOMSON, WILLIAM, son of William Thomson in Rumford,
Stirlingshire, settled as a farmer in Sandy, Utah, before 1881.
[NAS.SH.26.10.1881]

THOMPSON, WILLIAM, eldest son of John Thompson tailor,
White Hart Street, Dalkeith, Midlothian, died in Santa
Barbara, California, on 14 April 1882. [S#12,109]

THOMSON, ..., son of G. A. Thomson, was born in Racine,
Wisconsin, on 9 October 1863. [S#2611]

THOMSON, ..., son of Robert Thomson, was born in Portage City,
Wisconsin, on 9 June 1871. [S#8711]

THOMSON, ..., daughter of Robert Thomson, was born in Portage
City, Wisconsin, on 25 December 1872. [S#9179]

THORBURN, ALEXANDER, son of John Thorburn in Penicuik,
Midlothian, died in New Orleans in 1853. [S.16.7.1853]

THORBURN, ANDREW, in Detroit, died on 16 June 1849, cnf
1850 Edinburgh. [NAS.SC70.1.70]

THORBURN, JANETTE, born in 1850, daughter of William
Thorburn of Pennycuick, wife of David McLean,

Cummertrees, Dumfries-shire, died in Clarkson, Oakland
County, Michigan, in 1864. [AO]

THORSON, WILLIAM H., a poultry farmer in Windsor, Sonora
County, California, 1912. [NAS.RS.Forfar.77.271]

THWAITES, JANE, died in Salt Lake City, cnf 1895 Edinburgh.
[NAS.SC70.1.342]

TIBBETTS, GEORGE a clerk of the North Missouri Rail Road, son
of Alexander Tibbetts in Dumfries, died in St Louis in 1872.
[S#9089]

TINDALL, ...,son of James Tindall, was born in Plymouth
County, Iowa, on 2 March 1882. [S#12,071]

TOCHER, ALEXANDER, died in Colorado, cnf 1896 Edinburgh.
[NAS.SC70.1.348]

TOCHER, JOHN, born in 1871, son of William Tocher [1841-1909]
and Margaret Barclay [1844-1920], died in California during
1888. [Tyrie g/s, Aberdeenshire]

TODD, ALEXANDER, born 1819 in Houstoun, Renfrewshire, son
of Alexander Todd (1774-1851) and Martha Spiers (1776-
1846), settled in New Orleans. [Houstoun g/s]

TOD, MATTHEW, died in St Louis, cnf 1869 Edinburgh.
[NAS.SC70.1.141]

TOLMIE, Dr WILLIAM, manager of the Puget's Sound
Agricultural Society 1839. [DCB.XI.886]

TOP, MATTHEW, late butcher in the Middle Market of Edinburgh,
died at Rock Springs, St Louis, Missouri, on 16 August
1868. [S#7816]

TORRANCE, ROBERT B., born in Edinburgh 1813, died in San
Francisco on 11 December 1871. [S#8892]

TOUGH, DAVID, born in 1860, son of David Tough and Ann
Williams, died in New Mexico on 9 May 1891. [Eastern
Necropolis g/s, Dundee]

TOUGH, JAMES, son of James Tough, Mains of Drum, Drumoak, Aberdeenshire, died in St Louis, Missouri, on 18 June 1872. [AJ: 10.7.1872]

TOWERS, JAMES R., born 3 May 1839 in St Ninians, Stirlingshire, settled in Greene County, Iowa, by 1869, died 5 September 1921, buried in Highland Cemetery, Churdan, Greene County, Iowa. [IGS.HH.33.3.177]

TROTTER, GEORGE, from Dunbarton, died in Springfield, Illinois, 18 May 1842, cnf Edinburgh 1843.

TROTTER, WALTER, a mason from Lochgelly, Fife, emigrated with his wife and eight children to Illinois in 1847, perished on the journey. [FJ.23.9.1847]

TURNBULL, CATHERINE, in San Bernardino, California, cnf 1888 Edinburgh. [NAS.SC70.1.267]

TURNBULL, WILLIAM, of San Francisco, formerly a farmer in Lochend of Barra, Aberdeenshire, died in New York on 18 November 1869.[AJ:15.12.1869]

TURNER, DAVID DARLING, in Ascuncion parish, Louisiana, cnf Edinburgh 1901. [NAS.SC70.1.403/254]

TURNER, Mrs THOMAS, in Rapids parish, Louisiana, cnf 1901 Edinburgh. [NAS.SC70.1.403/244]

URE, JOHN, born in 1815, died in Oakland, California, on 12 May 1897. [Dunbarton g/s]

URQUHART, GEORGE, born in Ross-shire on 9 January 1846, son of Duncan Urquhart and Catherine McIntosh, married Helen Wood Sime in Perthshire on 22 June 1886, settled in Spokane, Washington, by 1888, later in Krupp, Washington, died in Marlin there during 1916. [WSP]

URQUHART, THOMAS, born 1773, a merchant, 'one of the first Scottish settlers on the banks of the Mississippi', died in New Orleans on 6 April 1841. [GSP#666]

URQUHART, THOMAS, a boy from New Orleans, was baptised in Ardrossan, Ayrshire, on 16 November 1785. [Ardrossan OPR]

VANCE, JANET, daughter of John Vance [1800-1867] and Janet
Aitken [1813-1890], wife of John Bryce, died in Astoria,
Oregon, on 8 April 1878. [Holy Rude g/s, Stirling]

VEITCH, ISOBELLA, born in 1866, third daughter of Robert
Veitch in Kingseat, Fife, died in St Louis on 30 July 1884.
[DJ]

VERT, FRANCIS DODS, born 1855, second son of Francis Vert, 9
Duncan Street, Newington, Edinburgh, late of Haddington,
East Lothian, died in Austin, Texas, on 11 July 1883.
[S#12,494]

VIAL, Mrs MARGARET, born in 1816, daughter of George
MacNaughten, Woodside, Aberdeen, died in Hazel Grove,
Illinois, on 18 May 1856.[AJ :18.6.1876]

WADDELL, GEORGE CHESHERS WILLIAMSON, from
Burntisland, Fife, settled in Denver, Colorado, cnf 1899
Edinburgh. [NAS.SC70.1.377/955]

WALKER, ANDREW, born 1860, a plasterer, son of Robert
Walker, tinsmith, 11 Sutherland Street, Edinburgh, died in
Chicago on 3 October 1883. [S#12,569]

WALKER, DAVID, from Fife, married Elizabeth Millar, eldest
daughter of George Millar, St Magdalen's, Perth, in Helena,
Arkansas, on 25 December 1875. [EC#28493][S#10,144]

WALKER, GEORGE C., son of Gabriel Walker, died in New
Orleans on 18 August 1851, cnf 1857 Edinburgh.
[W#11260][NAS.SC70.1.95]

WALKER, JAMES GRAY, born in 1851, son of William Walker
[1814-1893] and Margaret Gray [1815-1878], died in San
Francisco on 17 August 1891. [Grange g/s, Edinburgh]

WALKER, JOHN BLACK, possibly from Glasgow, settled in
Rockford, Illinois before 1877; nephew of Matthew Walker
a writer in Glasgow who died 10 March 1876.
[NAS.SH.19.12.1877; 13.3.1890]

WALKER, MARJORY, born in 1845, daughter of John Galen MD in Aberdeen, died in St Louis, Missouri, on 16 May 1870. [AJ: 8.6.1870]

WALKER, ROBERT, died in San Rafael, Marin County, California, cnf 1898 Edinburgh. [NAS.SC70.1.367/257]

WALKER, WILLIAM, infant son of James D. Walker, died in San Francisco on 26 July 1867. [S#7519]

WALKINGSHAW, ROBERT, born in 1858, from Helensburgh, Dunbartonshire, settled in Almaden, Santa Clara County, California, and in San Francisco. [GA#T-MR#10/1-4]

WALLACE, ANDREW, son of A. Wallace a farmer in Blairgreen, Saline, Fife, died at White Lake, Oakland County, Michigan, on 30 December 1842. [FH.9.3.1843]

WALLACE, GEORGE, from Ochiltree, Ayrshire, later in Springfield, Ohio, died in Sheridan, Kansas, on 17 December 1869. [S#8257]

WALLACE, HENRY, from Kettlebridge, Fife, married Isabella, second daughter of William Jinkens, from Burntisland, Fife, in Indianapolis, Indiana, on 11 May 1867. [S#7452]

WALLACE, JAMES, married Teennie Geddes, youngest daughter of Robert Geddes, both from Leith, in Chicago on 24 May 1883. [S#12,453]

WALLACE, JOHN JAMES, born 1851, from newton, Kirkpatrick Fleming, Dumfries-shire, died in Cleyton, California, on 23 May 1887. [AO: 26.8.1887]

WALLACE, ..., daughter of James Wallace, was born at West Law, Humboldt Park, Illinois, on 1 July 1884. [S#12800]

WALSH, JAMES ROBERTSON, married Marian Walker Moir daughter of James Moir of New York, in St Paul, Minnesota, on 22 May 1871. [S#8719]

WALSH, JOHN, in Sheridan, Wyoming, ca.1904. [UGL:UGD#91/232]

WARD, ELIZABETH WITTY, died in Platte, Cater, Nebraska, cnf 1893 Edinburgh. [NAS.SC70.1.322]

WARDROP, RICHARD, settled in St Louis, Missouri, by 1899, son of Jessie Whyte Glen or Wardrop who died 15 March 1886. [NAS.SH.2.11.1899]

WARRACK, ALEXANDER, born 1830, from New York, died in Little Rock, Arkansas, on 13 July 1878. [S#10,929]

WARRACK, ROBERT, born in 1827, from Aberdeen, died in Detroit on 30 March 1859. [AJ: 1.5.1859]

WATERS, ALEXANDER WILLIAM DUN, born 1863, elder son of James Waters of Glasgow and of Craigton, Stirlingshire, died in Le Mars, Iowa, on 22 March 1884. [S#12,702]

WATERSTON, ANDREW, in Westfield, Wisconsin, 1886. [NAS.RS.Forfar.45.31]

WATERSTON, DAVID, from Forfar, then in Weyanwega, Wanpeca County, Wisconsin, 1911. [NAS.RS.Forfar.76.191]

WATERSTON, DAVID E., in Perry, Ralls County, Missouri, 1913. [NAS.RS.Forfar.79.89]

WATERSTON, ERNEST, in Perry, Ralls County, Missouri, 1913. [NAS.RS.Forfar.79.89]

WATERSTON, THOMAS, in Perry, Ralls County, Missouri, 1913. [NAS.RS.Forfar.79.89]

WATKINS, ISABELLA, widow of James Watkins a merchant in Aberdeen, died in Detroit, Michigan, on 21 March 1876. [AJ: 5.5.1876]

WATSON, GEORGE, only son of James Watson from Edinburgh, died in Harrison, Kandiyohi County, Minnesota, on 13 January 1874. [S#9533]

WATSON, GEORGE, fifth son of Thomas Watson, Esperston, Midlothian, died in Forney, Kaufman County, Terxas, on 6 December 1881. [S#11,998]

WATSON, HENRY, son of Henry Watson a shipmaster in Dundee, a sailor in Downie Villa, California, by 1864. [NAS.SH.15.12.1864; 12.1.1865]

WATSON, HUGH, died in Crestfluie, Cherokee County, Kansas, cnf 1898. [NAS.SC70.1.370/708]

WATSON, JAMES, born 1800, son of James Watson (1778-1862) and Elizabeth Mustard (1806-1870), died in New Orleans in 1839. [St Aidan's g/s, Broughty Ferry]

WATSON, JAMES, son of Robert Watson, died in Detroit, Michigan, on 24 January 1848. [AJ#5285]

WATSON, JAMES, from Glasgow, married Avelina Osuna de Pomeroy from Sinaloa, Mexico, in San Francisco on 21 February 1881. [S#11844]

WATSON, JAMES, a farmer in Harlaw, Nebraska, cnf 1900 Edinburgh. [NAS.SC70.1.389/653]

WATSON, JOHN, a farmer in Clinton County, Iowa, married Annie Watson, daughter of James Watson in Bridge of Allan, Stirlingshire, there on 22 March 1870. [S#8316]

WATSON, ROBERT, late of Stoneywood, Aberdeenshire, died in Detroit, Michigan, on 11 March 1848, also his son James died there on 24 January 1849. [AJ#5285]

WATT, GEORGE DARLING, possibly from Kirkcudbrightshire, a reporter in Salt Lake City, Utah, by 1867. [NAS.SH.24.6.1867]

WATT, JAMES, born in 1834, eldest son of George Watt [died in 1887] and Helen Meikle [died in 1892], of Monastery Street, Dunfermline, Fife, a farmer in Comet, Kansas, married Margaret Kay, in Aitchison City, Kansas, on 27 June 1871, he died in Discord, Brown County, Kansas, on 29 March 1884. [DJ][Dunfermline g/s, Fife]

WATT, WILLIAM, possibly from Orkney, settled in Chicago by 1873. [NAS.SH.29.11.1873]

WATT, WILLIAM, Grass Valley, Nevada County, California, died on 6 July 1878. [S#10,934]

WATTIE, JAMES, born in 1850, son of James Wattie a merchant in Strathdon, Aberdeenshire, died in Parker, Kansas, on 27 August 1871. [AJ: 10.4.1872]

WAUGH, ROBERT, from Dunbar, East Lothian, married Susan Steel youngest daughter of George Steel in Chicago, there on 28 May 1872. [S#9011]

WEBBER, GEORGE WILLIAM, graduated MD from Glasgow University in 1888, died in Denver 22 May 1895. [RGG.636]

WEBSTER, FRANCIS, in San Francisco, 1908. [NAS.NRAS#1223]

WEDDERSPOON, ..., daughter of Thomas C. Wedderspoon, was born in Oakland, San Francisco, on 20 October 1875. [EC#28413]

WELLSTOOD, JOHN G., jr., of Company H, 28th Regiment of Connecticut Volunteers, son of John G. Wellstood in Greenwich, Connecticut, and grandson of John Wellstood in Edinburgh, died at Port Hudson, Louisiana, on 24 June 1863. [S#2551]

WELSH, DAVID, born in 1837, son of David Welsh [1799-1876] and Jane White [1799-1882], died in Washington on 26 September 1883. [Fettercairn g/s, Kincardineshire]

WELSH, GEORGE, born in 1828, late of Gorrenberry, Newcastleton, fourth son of James Welsh of Earlsheugh, died in David City, Nebraska, on 25 April 1891. [AO:15.5.1891]

WHITE, ALEXANDER CHARLES, son of James White a tenant farmer in Ayton Law, Berwickshire, settled in Woodbine, Kansas, by 1873.[NAS.SH.11.2.1873]

WHITE, ALEXANDER, born in Elgin, Morayshire, 1814, died in Rosedale, Lake Forest, Illinois, on 18 March 1872. [NAS.SH.23.6.1873]

WHITE, GEORGE, born in 1812, emigrated from Kirkpatrick-Fleming, Dumfries-shire, to New York in 1841, settled in

Lake County, Illinois, in 1844, died in Antioch, Illinois, on 22 February 1867. [AO]

WHITE, JANET, wife of James Little formerly of Bonshaw and Satur Mill, Dumfries-shire, died in Long Grove, Iowa, on 1 June 1898. [AO: 10.6.1898]

WHITE, JOHN CORBAT, in San Francisco by 1896, son of William White, a gardener in Selkirk, Peebles-shire, who died 4 February 1878. [NAS.SH.22.9.1896]

WHITELAW, DAVID, a seaman in Drycreek, California, who died in November 1850, cnf 1856 Edinburgh. [NAS.SC70.1.92/924]

WHITTON, ALEXANDER BARRY, in Detroit, cnf 1884 Edinburgh. [NAS.SC70.1.237/154]

WHITTON, JOHN, a surgeon in Iowa, died before 1870. [NAS.SH.19.7.1870]

WHITTON, WILFRED SMITH, born on 8 May 1863, son of Peter Whitton and Helen Isles, died in Denver, Colorado, on 27 July 1900. [Methven g/s, Perthshire]

WIGHT, ANDREW, possibly from Edinburgh, settled as a farmer in Madison County, Missouri, before 1831. [NAS.SH.2.2.1831]

WIGHTON, GEORGE, son of James Wighton (1767-1843) and Jean Watson (1768-1815), an engineer in New Orleans. [Old Mains g/s, Dundee]

WIGHTON, GEORGE DICKSON, son of William Wighton a watchmaker in Edinburgh, settled as a clerk in Colorado before 1881. [NAS.SH.2.11.1881]

WILKIE, JAMES, born 1799, third son of George Wilkie of Auchlishie, a merchant in New Orleans, died 18 August 1834. [Dundee g/s]

WILLIAMSON, ALEXANDER, from Northfield, Edinburgh, died in New Orleans on 3 October 1838, cnf 1852 Edinburgh. [NAS.SC70.1.75]

WILLIAMSON, ANDREW MELDRUM, in Melville, Wisconsin, by 1892, great grandson of James Williamson, shoemaker in Dunfermline, Fife, (died 1845). [NAS.SH.27.6.1892]

WILLIAMSON, BENJAMIN, eldest son of Captain Williamson of 5 Raeburn Place, Edinburgh, died in New Orleans in April 1841. [EEC#20224]

WILLIAMSON, DAVID, in Anthracite, Colorado, son of Robert Williamson in Ayr and his wife Agnes Stewart who died 22 December 1889. [NAS.SH.5.7.1897]

WILLIAMSON, JAMES HENRY, son of John Williamson, died in Folsom, California, on 11 November 1883. [S#12,577]

WILLIAMSON, SARAH, born in Dumfries-shire, died in Port Lobos, California, on 2 December 1884. [AO: 9.1.1885]

WILLIAMSON, WILLIAM, born in Kirkmaiden-in-Rhinns, Wigtownshire, on 22 July 1849, son of Reverend William Williamson and Mary McDowall, settled in Detroit. [F#2.342]

WILLIS, WILLIAM, born in 1841, only son of William Willis, died in Port Scott, Kansas, on 9 February 1873. [AO]

WILSON, ANNIE C., eldest daughter of William Wilson in Edmundstone Lodge, married Lachlan McLean of Menlo Park, at Russ House, San Mateo County, California, on 25 September 1877. [S#10,698]

WILSON, BETSY S., second daughter of David Wilson in Crossgates, Fife, married James H. Mason in Knightville, Clay County, Indiana, on19 June 1885. [DJ]

WILSON, DANIEL, born 1837, fifth son of Daniel Wilson, 5 Saunders Street, Stockbridge, Edinburgh, died in Detroit on 5 July 1869. [S#8111]

WILSON, DANIEL, born 1866, son of Charles Wilson [1842-1866], died in Detroit on 5 July 1898. [Dean g/s, Edinburgh]

WILSON, DAVID L., born 1807, settled in Nacogdoches, Texas, died at the Battle of the Alamo on 6 March 1836. [TSHA#25/0.536][DRTL]

WILSON, DAVID, jr., from Crossgates, Fife, married Isabella
Adamson, third daughter of John Adamson in Lochgelly,
Fife, in Knightville, Clay County, Indiana, on 2 September
1886. [PJ]

WILSON, ELIZABETH, daughter of Gabriel Wilson in
Musselburgh, and wife of Dr George Frederick Marnoch,
died in Los Elatus, Texas, on 8 September 1867. [S#7554]

WILSON, GEORGE, mason in Rockford, Illinois, 1893.
[NAS.RS.Nairn.18.212]

WILSON, HENRIETTA, in Rockford, Illinois, 1893.
[NAS.RS.Nairn.18.212]

WILSON, JAMES F., born 1789, eldest son of Alexander Wilson a
merchant in Inverness, settled in New Orleans, died in
Virginia on 5 October 1821. [BM#40.263][DPCA][SM]

WILSON, JAMES, son of Robert Wilson in Neuckfoot, settled as a
farmer in Wisconsin before 1852. [NAS.SH.13.1.1852]

WILSON, JAMES, born around 1845, youngest son of William
Wilson, Jinkabout Mill, Polmont, Stirlingshire, died in
Minneapolis East, Minnesota, on 1 April 1874.
[EC#27942][S#9594]

WILSON, JAMES, in Holy Cross, Dakota Territory, cnf 1874
Edinburgh. [NAS.SC70.1.169/595]

WILSON, Reverend JAMES KINNEAR, died in Wa-Reeney,
Trego County, Kansas, on 26 November 1879.
[EC#29711][S#11,363]

WILSON, JAMES, a farmer, youngest son of James Wilson a
manufacturer in Earlston, Berwickshire, married Ida Ophelia
Sawyers, eldest daughter of Holman Sawyers a cotton ginner
in Faurien County, Texas, at Kennedy Schoolhouse
Settlement on 11 December 1878. [EC#29412]

WILSON, JANE CONSTANT, born in 1828, daughter of James
Wilson a farmer from Bush, Lochmaben, Dumfries-shire,
died in Buffalo, Hart Grove, Sangamo County, Illinois, on 7
May 1866. [AO]

WILSON, JESSIE DARLING, fourth daughter of John Wilson, a bleacher in Dunfermline, married Dr Colonel William S. Scougal, a banker in Yankton, Dakota, youngest son of James Scougal, HM Inspector of Schools in Scotland, in New York on 16 October 1884. [S#12877]

WILSON, JOHN, a merchant skipper based in Lima, Peru, settled in Santa Barbara during the 1830s. [SHR#153/138]

WILSON, MATTHEW, eldest son of David Wilson in Crossgates, Fife, married Mary Elizabeth Elson in Rockville Park, Indiana, on 8 October 1885. [PJ]

WILSON, MARY, youngest daughter of William Wilson, Poughkeepsie, NY, married James Freeman Gibbs, Sandwich, Massachusetts, in New Orleans on 12 July 1871. [S#8748]

WILSON, PETER, born 1826, died in Wesley, Illinois, on 9 May 1882. [Wigtown g/s]

WILSON, THOMAS, from Dalton, Dumfries-shire, settled in Chicago by 1854, married Mary Gibson (1825-1854). [Dalton g/s]

WILSON, THOMAS H., son of John Wilson [1805-1869] and Margaret Hood [1815-1908], settled in Eaton, Colorado. [Lintrathen g/s, Angus]

WILSON, THOMAS, an ironfounder from Dunfermline, Fife, died in Madeira, Minnesota, on 11 April 1887. [DJ: 7.5.1887]

WILSON, WILLIAM, died in Rochford, Illinois, on 12 September 1873. [NAS.SH.3.5.1883]

WILSON, ..., daughter of Samuel W. W. Wilson, was born at Stearus Prairie, Nebraska, on 3 December 1877. [S#10,744]

WILSON, ..., daughter of Reverend J. A. Wilson, was born in St Louis on 9 November 1879. [S#11,344]

WISHART, GEORGE, son of George Wishart in Howaback, Sandwick, Orkney, settled in Kansas before 1873. [NAS.SH.3.11.1873]

WOOD, ANNIE CAMERON, wife of Robert Caldwell a civil engineer, died in Decorah, Iowa, on 7 January 1881. [S#11,724]

WOOD, GEORGE, in De Kalb, Illinois, by 1899, son of Robert Wood in Whitecraig, Inveresk, who died 28 April 1846. [NAS.SH.25.7.1899]

WOOD, or CAVERS, HELEN, in Village Creek, Iowa, daughter of James Wood in Ancrum and his wife Jane Thomson who died 14 August 1891. [NAS.SH.7.10.1896]

WOOD, THOMAS, born 1812, second son of John Wood a shipbuilder in Dunbar, East Lothian, died in Louisiana on 15 January 1875. [S#9844]

WOTHERSPOON, JOHN, graduated MB, CM, in 1889 at Glasgow University, settled in Seattle, Washington. [RGG.659]

WREY, GEORGE, in the Rocky Mountains 1876, to grow vines in California 1883. [NAS.GD21.482-4]

WRIGHT, or MORRIS, JANET S., in Washington, Iowa, 1875. [NAS.SC58.59.28.159]

WRIGHT, MAXWELL, in Cook County, Illinois, died in London, cnf Edinburgh 1901. [NAS.SC70.1.408/132]

WYLIE, JAMES, in Toledo, America, second son of Alexander Wylie a distiller in Campbeltown, Argyll, married Jane Greenlees, eldest daughter of William Greenlees a farmer in Ardnacross, Argyll, in Harlem, Winnebago County, Illinois, on 18 December 1851. [W#1301]

WYLLIE, JAMES, in Washington 1858. [NAS.SC49.48.25.58.267]

WYLLIE, WILLIAM, born 1839, son of George Wyllie, died in Clyde, Kansas, 25 June 1873. [Wigtown g/s]

WYLLIE, WILLIAM FLEMING, probably from Ayrshire, settled as a farmer in Utica, Illinois, before 1879. [NAS.SH.16.8.1879]

YEAMAN, JAMES, born in Oathlaw, Angus, on 15 September 1845, son of Robert Yeaman and Susan Scott, "sometime in California", died in Dundee on 1 December 1906. [Oathlaw g/s, Angus]

YEAMAN, WILLIAM, born in Annan, Dumfries-shire, during 1847, died in San Francisco on 12 November 1898. [AO: 9.12.1898]

YEATS, WILLIAM, son of Peter Yeats in Aberdeen, died in St Louis, Missouri, on 9 November 1878. [AJ: 5.12.1878]

YORK, RICHARD, born in 1826, son of William York, a builder in Glasgow, and Janet Masterton, drowned in the Mississippi River in 1855. [Necropolis g/s, Glasgow]

YOUNG, ANDREW JAMES, a farmer in Red Oak, Michigan, by 1899, possibly from Ayrshire. [NAS.SH.30.11.1899]

YOUNG, CATHERINE, born 1864, wife of William A. Young, daughter of John Thomson, grand-daughter of William Thomson in Gretna, Dumfries-shire, died at Poncha Springs, Colorado, on 12 June 1887. [AO:8.7.1887]

YOUNG, CHRISTIAN, daughter of Reverend James Young in Dunfermline, Fife, wife of Alexander D. Spence, died in Fresno, California, on 14 February 1910. [FH]

YOUNG, FRANK STANLEY, graduated MA from Glasgow University in 1890, an accountant and financial agent in Kansas City. [RGG.665]

YOUNG, GEORGE, in Minnesota, by 1892, son of John Young and Helen Drysdale (died 9 April 1852) in Dunfermline, Fife. [NAS.SH.8.6.1892]

YOUNG, HUGH, a merchant, second son of James Young the sheriff substitute of Kincardineshire, died in New Orleans on 5 February 1833. [AJ#4449]

YOUNG, JAMES, son of George Young a Lieutenant of the Royal Navy in Portsoy, Banffshire, died in St Louis on 9 December 1848. [AJ#5276]

YOUNG, JAMES, son of Archibald Young and Janet Brown in Dundee, a seaman in California by 1871. [NAS.SH.10.5.1871]

YOUNG, JAMES, a merchant in Canton, Minnesota, by 1892, son of John Young and Helen Drysdale (died 9 April 1852) in Dunfermline, Fife.[NAS.SH.8.6.1892]

YOUNG, JAMES CHARLES, second son of Hume Young, died in Alleghany, California, on 4 January 1872. [S#8932]

YOUNG, or STURGEON, JANE, in Minnesota, by 1892, daughter of John Young and Helen Drysdale (died 9 April 1852) in Dunfermline, Fife.[NAS.SH.8.6.1892]

YOUNG, JOHN, in Minnesota by 1892, son of John Young and Helen Drysdale (died 9 April 1852) in Dunfermline, Fife.[NAS.SH.8.6.1892]

YOUNG, Reverend JOHN, in Greenfield, Iowa, by 1899, son of John Young, a labourer in Bathgate, West Lothian, who died 22 December 1894. [NAS.SH.2.10.1899]

YOUNG, ROBERT, born 1844, son of James Young and Margaret Martin, died in Tacoma, USA, 31 January 1889. [Montrose, Rosehill, g/s]

YOUNG, THOMAS, born in 1847, died in Joplin, Missouri, on 5 September 1873. [Dunlop g/s, Ayrshire]

YOUNG, WILLIAM B., born in 1856, son of James Young and Fanny Turton, died in California on 2 March 1903. [Blairgowrie g/s, Perthshire]

YULE, ALEXANDER, born in 1794, from Meikle Rathen, Aberdeenshire, died in Wisconsin on 29 May 1868. [AJ: 15.7.1868]

YULE, Mrs ANN, born in 1781, widow of John Yule, from Burnside, Craigievar, Aberdeenshire, died in Virginia Grove, Iowa, on 9 January 1861. [AJ: 27.2.1861]

YULE, JESSIE, born in 1836, daughter of Alexander Gibson in Aberdeen, died in Kenosha, Wisconsin, on 23 June 1854. [AJ: 18.10.1854]

YULE, ROBERT, from New Orleans, married Janet Webster, eldest daughter of Andrew Webster, Scoonie Bridge, Leven, Fife, in Edinburgh on 21 July 1873. [EC#27707]

YULE, SAMUEL, from Aberdeenshire, settled in Ashland County, Ohio, during 1836, moved to Red Oak, Indiana, in 1837. [ENES#1.252]